Minorities in the Ottoman Empire

Minorities in the Ottoman Empire

Edited by

MOLLY GREENE

Markus Wiener Publishers
Princeton

Reprinted from *Princeton Papers: Interdisciplinary Journal of Middle Eastern Studies*, Volume XII, 2005

For information, write to: Markus Wiener Publishers
231 Nassau Street, Princeton, NJ 08542
www.markuswiener.com

Cover illustrations, clockwise from top left: Headdress worn by Christian and Jewish women in Diyarbekir; headgear of Greek priests, usually made of black felt; turban worn by some Greek merchants in the Archipelago; headdress worn by Greek women in Anatolia (visible only indoors, because it is covered by a veil when the women leave the home). From Antoine Laurant Castellan (1772–1838), *Moeurs, usages, costumes des Othomans, et abrégé de leur histoire*, vol. 6. Paris: Nepveu, Lib. . . ., 1812. Used by permission of the Rare Books Division, Department of Rare Books and Special Collections, Princeton University Library.

Library of Congress Cataloging-in-Publication Data
Minorities in the Ottoman Empire / Molly Greene, editor.
   p. cm.
Includes bibliographical references.
  ISBN 978-1-55876-228-2 (pbk.)
  1. Minorities—Turkey—History—18th century. 2. Minorities—Turkey—History—19th century. 3. Turkey—History—18th century. 4. Turkey—History—19th century.
I. Greene, Molly, 1959–
  DR434.M56 2003
  956.1'015'08693—dc21

                           2003008665

Contents

Introduction

MOLLY GREENE

> The leading merchants of the town, after they had placed the
> people in the houses, Turkish in Turkish homes and Christian
> and Jewish in Christian homes, gathered in the great ground-
> floor room of Hadji Ristić's house. There were the *mukhtars*
> (the Moslem leaders) and the *kmets* (the Christian headmen) of
> all the quarters, exhausted and wet to the skin, after having wak-
> ened and moved to safe quarters all their fellow citizens. Turks,
> Christians and Jews mingled together. The force of the elements
> and the weight of common misfortune brought all these men
> together and bridged, at least for this one evening, the gulf that
> divided one faith from the other.
>
> —Ivo Andrić, *The Bridge on the Drina*

So runs Ivo Andrić's fictional account of one Bosnian town's response to a
crippling flood in the second half of the eighteenth century, by which time
Bosnia had been under Ottoman rule for three hundred years. Although Andrić's famous epic of life in Višegrad is a work of fiction, his book, and this

1

passage in particular, picks up on one of the most important themes in the historiography of the Christians and Jews of the Ottoman Empire.

Certainly the overwhelming emphasis in the literature has been on communal autonomy and the centrality of the religious divide, institutionalized in the *millet* system. The conviction of communal autonomy has encouraged the study of the Jewish and Christian communities (whether Orthodox, Maronite, Armenian, or other) as self-contained entities. This approach often enlists the community in the service of nationalist historiography. Examples of such "communal histories" are too vast to even begin to relate.

Andrić's account can be seen as an imaginative representation of that model: even in the middle of a flood, the boundary of religion, "the gulf that divided one faith from the other," within the town was maintained. But there is more to the story than that. If the common folk were carefully herded to the appropriate shelter, the religious leadership of the town—Muslim, Christian, and Jewish—gathered together in the capacious home of a leading citizen to wait out the storm together. Here Andrić's description raises questions that have received less attention. What circumstances brought the religious communities together and how was the interaction managed? How were boundaries constructed and maintained in situations of social fluidity? Andrić's account suggests one approach, which was differential treatment according to class. Interfaith mingling was a prerogative (or perhaps a duty) of the elite, something not allowed those further down the social scale.

Andrić's description is also suggestive because it treats the management of religious diversity with scant regard for formal institutions. Ottoman historians have been inclined to think about religious diversity in terms of institutions imposed by the state. Thus Benjamin Braude and Bernard Lewis, in their now-classic *Christians and Jews in the Ottoman Empire: The Functioning of a Plural Society*, emphasize the role of the Ottoman sultans (and, more broadly, Muslim states) in creating communal autonomy. The Ottomans, we read, "created a society which allowed a great degree of communal autonomy." A rather fixed notion of Islamic law is also emphasized when thinking about relations between Muslims and non-Muslims: "The weakness or strength of the Muslim state, and, more generally, the relations between Islam and the outside world, affected the strict enforcement or lax disregard of the restrictions mandated by the Holy Law."[1] This approach has had the effect of suggesting that the history of the religious communities is the history of the institutions and the laws that were directed at them.

The four essays in this volume, all of them concerned with the eighteenth and nineteenth centuries, ask different questions and choose different emphases. The first three essays, by Socrates Petmezas, Fatma Müge Göçek, and Najwa al-Qattan, explore the unknown terrain that falls between the internal life of the community and the formal structures that linked the non-Muslims to the state. The final essay is also the last in terms of chronology. With its focus on the second half of the nineteenth century, it is very much part of the debate over the relationship between westernization, reform, and secularism. Rodrigue demonstrates that Jewish reformers were not necessarily either secular or bent on importing western forms and values.

In discussing how Jews and Christians actually navigated daily life in the Empire in the post-classical period, we hope to include non-Muslims in some of the more exciting trends in Ottoman historiography today. An older paradigm—the "decline" thesis—tended to view the seventeenth and eighteenth centuries through the binary opposition of purity and corruption: institutions which had once been pure were now corrupt. This model is implied above, where only two legal situations are possible: "strict enforcement" or "lax disregard" of the restrictions mandated by the Holy Law. Recent writing, on provincial, gender, and legal history in particular, has placed new emphasis on the successful management of change, including a positive assessment of the increased ability of social actors to negotiate with representatives of the state, and informal power. In her book on Mosul, Dina Khoury demonstrates how local elite families were able to take advantage of Mosul's position as an important frontier city, lying near the border with Iran. They carved out a niche for themselves through control of revenue collection and supply of the army. Unlike earlier writing on provincial history, which equated a rise in local power with a decline at the center, Khoury emphasizes negotiation between Istanbul and Mosul and stresses that Mosuli elites were still closely bound to the imperial city.[2] Jane Hathaway strikes a similar theme for Ottoman Egypt in this period. She focuses on the rise of the Egyptian variant of what she calls "an empire-wide military and administrative culture based on households" that linked provinces to the center in new, but still effective, ways.[3] Turning to the Balkans, Eleni Gara's work on communal organization in (today's) northern Greece shows that informal institutions were both durable and effective. She acknowledges that the Ottoman legal system did not formally recognize communal corporations. But, she continues, "this does not mean that Ottoman administrators ignored the phenomenon. To the contrary, recent research based on judicial records has shown that the Ottoman court not only tolerated communal corporations, but was very well able to reconcile this reality with Islamic law."[4] Recent studies focused more directly on Ottoman legal culture have also drawn our attention to flexibility, evolution, and negotiation. Judith Tucker's study of Syrian and Palestinian courts and Leslie Pierce's work on one extraordinary case in Aintab both emphasize flexibility and responsiveness of the legal system, as well as the importance of individual agency.[5]

The first essay in this volume is Socrates Petmezas' "Christian Communities in Eighteenth and Early Nineteenth Century Ottoman Greece: Their Fiscal Functions." Petmezas is one of a number of younger scholars writing today in Greece, which has become, in recent years, one of the liveliest sites for Ottoman historiography. The institutional approach to Ottoman history that I described above used to be dominant in Greece as well, but Greek scholars had their own reasons for this preference. They were not interested in the purity or corruption of Ottoman institutions. Rather, as nationalist historians, they wanted to emphasize the strength, stability, and legitimacy of certain institutions—primarily the Church, the *millet* system, and the rural communities—which, in their view, preserved and nurtured the nation. Challenges to these authorities, when noted at all, were viewed with disfavor. As we shall see in this volume, Petmezas rejects this interpretation of the rural communities. In other work he has done, he has started to dismantle the myth of the Greek Orthodox Church as the sole legitimate representative of the Orthodox Christians of the Empire and thus a natural protector of the Nation. For several centuries following 1453, Petmezas shows, successive patriarchs had to struggle hard to impose their authority on and maintain the loyalty of bishops who, often as not, considered their primary allegiance to be to the sultan rather than to the patriarch.[6] Paraskevas Konortas, another Greek scholar, has established that Ottoman "ecclesiastical" documents did not use the term "millet" vis-à-vis the Christians in the early centuries of Ottoman rule. The full institutional and legal development of the millet was not complete until the second half of the nineteenth century.[7]

Petmezas' chapter has a dual purpose. The first is to collect and assess the existing data on local (communal and *kaza*) finances in selected eighteenth-century Greek communities. Using these data, he then analyzes the fiscal functions of territorial communities, both rural and urban. Petmezas discusses a number of different communities from both mainland and insular Greece and meticulously exploits a wealth of data produced by the communities themselves.

Petmezas devotes a good deal of attention to the upland community of Zagora, on Mount Pelion in eastern Thessaly.[8] Throughout the Empire in the late seventeenth and the eighteenth century, changing fiscal practices allowed for the increased participation of local elites in the farming and collection of taxes. Petmezas links this development directly to the consolidation of communal administration in Zagora and other Greek communities of the time (p. 81). Thus it is not a coincidence that the community began to keep a register of communal finances, now stored in the municipal library in Zagora, in the middle of the eighteenth century. This register grew more sophisticated and thorough, as the commune grew in strength, to the point where we now possess an almost complete series of balance sheets for the years 1783–1822. These balance sheets neatly record revenues and expenses for every fiscal year and also provide a complete list of all creditors to the community (p. 87).

Using these and similar records from other communities, Petmezas breaks the oft-made link between Ottoman "decline" (a term he rejects) and the growth of Greek nationalism and shows instead that the growing strength of Christian communal government must be explained in fiscal/administrative, rather than in national, terms. In tracing the development of communal fiscal management, he also addresses major themes in the historiography of the eighteenth-century Ottoman Empire, such as the local elites (*ayan*), tax-farming, provincial unrest, and the fate of the peasantry, and links them to the history of the Christian communities in the Balkans.

Several of the communities in Petmezas' study clearly enjoyed high levels of autonomy in the eighteenth century. The whole point of the two sets of books that the Zagoriot elite developed—one for the Ottomans, one for the community—was to keep the Ottoman tax collector at bay, which they did quite successfully. This fits in nicely with the *millet* model of Ottoman society. But Petmezas does not take the community for granted. Instead he suggests why some communities were able to maintain their independence, in terms of controlling access *as a community* to collective resources, while others met the fate of widespread peasant expropriation by local elites. The Christian elites, the *kocabaşıs*, play a very particular role in this story. The *kocabaşıs* have been reviled in Greek nationalist historiography as "Christian Turks" bent on exploiting the peasantry. Petmezas shows instead that, unlike Muslim local elites, the *kocabaşıs* depended on the internal coherence of the community for their social, economic, and political power in Ottoman society (p. 85). While the *kocabaşıs* certainly benefited from their position as administrators of communal finances, they were careful not to push their financial advantage to the point of peasant expropriation. Petmezas' article, like Beshara Doumani's recent book *Rediscovering Palestine: Merchants and Peasants in Jabal Nablus 1700–1900*, shows a new interest among Ottoman historians in understanding how rural communities shaped their own destinies.[9]

Fatma Müge Göçek also writes on the eighteenth century, but with her essay we move from the Balkan countryside to Istanbul, the imperial capital. Her subject is the recourse of Ottoman Christians and Jews to the Islamic court. The topic is one that has long interested scholars working on the non-Muslims of the Ottoman Empire, who have tended to argue that non-Muslims used the *kadı* court as a notary public more than as a judicial arbiter. Benjamin Braude, for example, in his article on commercial life in the Balkans in the sixteenth and seventeenth centuries, writes that Jewish and Christian businessmen wanted to have a legally recognized document in case a civil or criminal action against them was brought to the *kadı*.[10]

Göçek read over seven hundred cases from the Islamic court in Galata (there were sixteen such courts in Istanbul in the eighteenth century). She chose Galata because it contained both Islamic and communal courts. Therefore, recourse to the Islamic court cannot be explained by a lack of Christian or Jewish judicial institutions.

Göçek's approach is both dynamic and comparative. She points out that, over the course of the century, the number of Armenians and Greeks appearing in court showed a radical increase. Jews, on the other hand, are almost entirely absent from the court records. Nearly all the cases concern inheritance; the few that do not are property disputes and sales.

The author is careful to contextualize her findings. A crisis in the leadership of the Greek community in the second half of the eighteenth century may help explain the "explosion" in the number of Greeks appearing in the Galata court after 1763 (p. 61). At the same time, Göçek suggests an enduring distinction between the Greeks and the Armenians on the one hand, and the Jewish community on the other. The Jewish communal leaders, she argues, exercised more effective social control over individual Jews than did the Armenian or Greek leadership over their parishioners (p. 60).

This conclusion suggests several things. First, it is unsatisfactory to interpret Christian recourse to the Islamic courts as a sort of protection against Muslim power since, if that were the case, we would expect to see Jews in court as often as Christians. Second, in trying to understand the strength of communal autonomy in the Ottoman Empire, it is not enough to concern oneself with the arrangements worked out between the state and community leaders. Clearly individuals could, and did, exercise their own agency. In this sense Göçek's essay is in line with recent writing on Ottoman legal history, which emphasizes the agency of individuals and the flexibility of the court system.[11] Finally, there is something to be gained by considering the long-term history of each community, rather than thinking in terms of a shared non-Muslim status. Recent work by Greek scholars, building on Braude's observations from twenty years ago, continues to dismantle the historiographical edifice of a powerful Greek Orthodox church hierarchy established in 1453 and enduring until some point in the nineteenth century.[12] This suggests that the Orthodox church continued to suffer from marginality in the Ottoman period, much as it had (to varying degrees depending upon the period) under the Byzantines. This marginality seems to have translated into less effective community leadership in a way that was not true for the Jews. Further research should aim to relate the internal dynamics of the non-Muslim communities to the place of the Jewish or Christian individual in Ottoman society.

With Najwa al-Qattan's chapter we retain the urban focus but move to the Arab provinces, specifically Damascus from the mid-eighteenth to the mid-nineteenth century. This essay, like Göçek's, relies on the records of the *kadı* court in Damascus, but al-Qattan is using her source to rethink ideas about urban segregation along religious lines. Although Ottoman cities (and Islamic cities in general) were free of legal segregation, historians agree that various factors—al-Qattan cites a strong sense of religious identification, communal organization, and sectarian sensitivities and prejudice—gave rise to predominantly Christian and Jewish neighborhoods. In Damascus, the majority of Christians lived in the Christian quarters of Bab Sharqi and Bab Tuma (which the court refers to collectively as Mahallat al-Nasara, the Christian quarters) and the Jews lived in Mahallat al-Yahud (p. 14). The court documents reveal, however, that a number of Muslims lived in these neighborhoods and that Christians and Jews could also be found in predominantly Muslim quarters. Thus it is reasonable to ask, as al-Qattan does, just how Christian was the Christian quarter? The author, in other words, is not content to accept formal characterizations. Instead she shows that the neat categories used by the court, and adopted by historians, mask a more complex reality.

Al-Qattan goes beyond an analysis of home ownership to look at several other aspects of the real estate market as well. There was clearly a lively, although not very lucrative, speculative market in buildings. Both Muslim and Christian speculators were active in the real-estate market in the Christian quarter, selling to Christian buyers. In fact, she concludes, most Muslim real estate speculation was centered on Christian buyers in the Christian areas (p. 26). This suggests an open and dynamic market.

Shared housing arrangements and sales of shares in a house were common. The latter was due in part to the legacy of complex Islamic inheritance laws, but also to a lack of affordable housing. Not only was partial ownership widespread, but house-sharing crossed sectarian lines. Al-Qattan is not disputing the existence of sectarian divides. But the reality of constant and intense contact across religious divides, for at least some part of the Damascene population, suggests that historians need to reassess, not so much sectarian divides themselves, but "the way in which such divides played themselves out in daily life" (p. 32).

The final chapter in this book focuses on an individual rather than a community. Aron Rodrigue's contribution looks at the life of the educator Barukh ben Isaac Mitrani, who was active in Edirne, the city of his birth, in the second half of the nineteenth century. Mitrani was an energetic participant in the conflicts that were roiling the Jewish community at this time. He taught Hebrew in the local school founded by Joseph Halevi, the noted figure of the Jewish Enlightenment (Haskalah), and engaged in polemics in the emerging

Sephardi Jewish press. Despite his support for modern education, and his enlightened outlook on a wide range of issues, Mitrani came into serious conflict with the Edirne branch of that ardent proponent of Jewish enlightenment, the Alliance Israélite Universelle. Mitrani felt modern education should strengthen Judaism, not weaken it as he said the Alliance was doing. Messianic ideas, Rodrigue argues, combined with Haskalah into "the fledgling movement of religious Zionism" (p. 129). Mitrani welcomed the emancipation of the Jews in Europe, not as a harbinger of a new secular order where Jews could be full citizens, but as a sign that the messianic era was at hand.

Rodrigue's observations on Mitrani, which echo those he made in his full-length study of Jewish education in the Ottoman Empire in the nineteenth century, *French Jews, Turkish Jews: The Alliance Israélite Universelle and the Politics of Jewish Schooling in Turkey, 1860–1925*, speak to the relationship between secularism and reform. The reformist impulse, it has often been argued (or assumed), whether the Tanzimat of the Ottoman government, or reforms by leaders in the various communities, was essentially a secular one. Conversely, opposition to reform has been framed as religious fanaticism, particularly on the part of Muslims. This picture is slowly being complicated by scholars of the nineteenth century. Ussama Makdisi, in his study of nineteenth-century Lebanon, has gone so far as to suggest that that Ottoman Tanzimat actually facilitated, albeit unwittingly, the intrusion of religion into the public sphere of politics.[13] Tanyus Shahin, the muleteer who led the 1860 revolt that forms the centerpiece of Makdisi's book, was both an ardent Christian and a fervent supporter of the Tanzimat. Similarly, Mitrani effortlessly combines messianism with loyalty to many of the ideas of the Jewish enlightenment. Rodrigue mentions that the Jews of the Ottoman European provinces must have been affected by Balkan nationalism. Future research would do well to consider the Jews in this comparative Balkan context.

Years ago, in his debate with Stanford Shaw over the nature of Balkan society under Ottoman rule, the eastern European historian Wayne Vucinich characterized the Ottoman system as "a ramshackle empire which was bound to fall to pieces once the overwhelming police power crumbled."[14] Revealingly, Vucinich goes on to explain that this was so because the Ottoman system failed to develop a sense of belonging in the minds of its subjects. Clearly, it is no longer satisfactory (if it ever was) to say that the Ottoman Empire owed its centuries-long existence to police power. Ottoman historians, accordingly, have begun to consider the construction and maintenance of authority and consensus, alongside the deployment of naked force. If the possibility of Ottoman authority has been too hastily dismissed, the authority of the communities has been too quickly endorsed. The Christian and Jewish communities within the Ottoman Empire have enjoyed an enduring image as fortresses that effectively sheltered and disciplined their followers who, in turn, submitted themselves to the authority of their communal leaders. Without denying the reality of community sentiment, this model is insufficient. It cannot explain, for example, how and why, in Damascus, a Christian daughter would seek the assistance of the Muslim court in evicting her mother from her home so that she could put the house on the market. This is just one anecdote, but it points to a larger truth that the essays in this collection have borne in mind.[15] Communal authority and solidarity in the Ottoman Empire were the product of human effort. Like all human creations, they were fragile constructs that had to be renewed and defended with every generation.

Notes

1. Pp. 10 and 1. Daniel Goffman's important article, "Ottoman Millets in the Early Seventeenth Century," *New Perspectives on Turkey* 11 (1994), maintains the focus on state policy toward non-Muslims.

2. Dina Khoury, *State and Provincial Society in the Ottoman Empire: Mosul 1540–1834* (Cambridge: Cambridge University Press, 1997).

3. Hathaway emphasizes the mediating abilities of the household, which grew in importance in the seventeenth and eighteenth centuries. The household of an Ottoman official in Egypt, she writes, "served as a meeting ground for imperial and local interests." Jane Hathaway, *The Politics of Households in Ottoman Egypt: The Rise of the Qazdaglis* (Cambridge: Cambridge University Press, 1997), pp. 1 and 21.

4. Eleni Gara, "In Search of Communities in Seventeenth Century Ottoman Sources: The Case of the Kara Ferye District," *Turcica* 30 (1998), pp. 138–39.

5. Judith Tucker, *In the House of the Law: Gender and Islamic Law in Ottoman Syria and Palestine* (Berkeley: University of California Press, 1998), and Leslie Peirce, "Le Dilemme de Fatma: Crime Sexuel et Culture Juridique dans une Cour Ottomane au Début des Temps Modernes," *Annales: Histoire, Sciences Sociales* 53, no. 2 (1998): 291–319.

6. Paolo Odorico, with the collaboration of S. Adrachas, T. Karanastassis, K.

Kostis, and S. Petmezas, *Conseils et mémoires de Synadinos, prêtre de Serrès en Macédoine (XVIIe Siècle)* (Paris: Editions de l'Association "Pierre Belon," 1996). This volume includes the Greek original, as well as the French translation, of the memoirs of an Orthodox priest of the seventeenth century. Several essays introduce the memoir. It is in his essay entitled "L'Organisation Ecclèsiastique sous la domination Ottomane" that Petmezas discusses the fractious bishops, p. 492.

7. Paraskevas Konortas, "From Tâ'ife to Millet: Ottoman Terms for the Ottoman Greek Orthodox Community," in Dimitri Gondicas and Charles Issawi, eds., *Ottoman Greeks in the Age of Nationalism* (Princeton: Darwin Press, 1999).

8. This area was the subject of his Ph.D. dissertation, *Recherches sur l'Économie et les Finances des villages du Pélion, région d'industries rurales, ca. 1750–1850* (E.H.E.S.S: Paris, 1989).

9. Amy Singer's book, *Palestinian Peasants and Ottoman Officials: Rural Administration around Sixteenth-century Jerusalem* (Cambridge: Cambridge University Press, 1994), is concerned with the same question but for an earlier period, the sixteenth century, when rural elites were much less prominent.

10. Benjamin Braude, "Venture and Faith in the Commercial Life of the Ottoman Balkans, 1500–1650," *International History Review* 7, no. 4 (1985): 519–42.

11. See especially Leslie Peirce's article cited in note 2.

12. S. Petmezas, "L'Organisation ecclésiastique sous la domination Ottomane," in P. Odorico, ed., *Conseils et mémoires de Synadinos, prêtre de Serrès en Macédoine (XVIIe siècle)* (Paris: Editions de l'Association "Pierre Belon," 1996). See also note 6 above.

13. Ussama Makdisi, *The Culture of Sectarianism: Community, History, and Violence in Nineteenth-Century Ottoman Lebanon* (Berkeley: University of California Press, 2000).

14. Wayne Vucinich, "Reply," *Slavic Review* 21 (December 1962): 638.

15. The case of the eviction is not the only one where *dhimmi*s involved the Islamic court in their family matters. Najwa al-Qattan comments (p. 42) that "it was apparently not uncommon for some *dhimmi*s to misrepresent either the law or their own family relationships in fraudulent attempts to inherit from others."

Across the Courtyard: Residential Space and Sectarian Boundaries in Ottoman Damascus

NAJWA AL-QATTAN

Introduction

In September 1780 Fransis w. Yusuf al-Rassi, a Christian man, bought from Isma'il al-Halabi b. Darwish a house in the Christian quarter of Damascus. Isma'il made 500 *qurush*. For his part, Fransis acquired a new home and an interesting mix of neighbors: a Muslim, a Christian, and a Jew.[1] As will become evident from this paper, this mixture of neighbors was not unusual in late-eighteenth-century Damascus, but neither was it an everyday occurrence. What did take place daily, however, was the appearance of men and women at the Muslim court (*mahkama*) to register property sales.

Historians using the *sijill* records of the Muslim *shari'a* courts in Ottoman Syria have often noted the somewhat disappointing overabundance of cases pertaining to real estate transactions. In Damascus, for example, it appears that men and women spent a considerable portion of their time at the Muslim court selling, buying, renting, and litigating over real estate: residences, shops and other commercial establishments, parcels of land, and the establishing, maintaining, and renting of *waqf* (pious foundation) properties are the object of perhaps 80% of the courts' business. This study, for which a total of seventy-eight *sijill* registers have been consulted, uses this material to focus on Damascene Christians and the patterns of their residential distribution from the mid-eighteenth to the mid-nineteenth centuries.[2]

Residential patterns, neighborhood distribution, and property ownership among the Ottoman Empire's various urban populations both Muslim and *dhimmi* (non-Muslim) have been studied before.[3] Historians agree that minorities, religious and otherwise, were not legally confined to segregated urban areas in the manner of Europe's medieval Jewry. Nonetheless, many also agree that in many Ottoman urban centers a strong sense of religious identification, communal self-organization, and sectarian sensitivities and prejudice gave shape to predominantly Christian and Jewish neighborhoods where *dhimmi*s lived and where they had in place their religious and communal institutions such as churches and schools.

During the period under study, the residential distribution of Damascene *dhimmi*s appears to follow this general pattern. The majority of Christians lived in the Christian quarters of Bab Sharqi and Bab Tuma and the Jews in Maḥallat al-Yahud (the Jewish quarter). However, the composition and boundaries of *dhimmi* and other neighborhoods changed over time. Although the *sijill* registers consistently refer to the Christian and Jewish areas of the city as Maḥallat al-Naṣara and Maḥallat al-Yahud respectively, the registers also make evident that a noticeable number of Muslims lived in these areas just as Christians and Jews crossed sectarian lines to dwell in the quarters of Qaymariyya, Kharab, and Maydan/Bab al-Musalla.

The confessional segmentation of urban space raises several issues. First, *dhimmi* neighborhoods retained their *dhimmi*-specific names even as their inhabitants came and went and even as it also becomes apparent from the registers that their boundaries were fluid. To what extent, for example, was the Christian quarter Christian?[4] Second, how do we categorize neighborhoods such as Qaymariyya, Kharab, and Maydan with their relatively substantial Christian populations and their "Muslim" coloration?

Third, as Antoine Abdel Nour has pointed out, notions of city quarters and neighborhoods appear to be complex. According to him the quarter (*hara*) represented the basic administrative unit of the city. Each *hara* comprised a number of *zuqaq*s (alleys, both closed and open), but also was part of a larger city-wide organizational hierarchy in which several *hara*s comprised a *mahalla* (or *hayy*) and several *mahalla*s in turn were part of the eight divisions (*athman*, literally, eighths) into which Damascus was divided and which included its intra- and extramural quarters.[5] Most importantly, Abdel Nour has noted that Ottoman judicial and fiscal authorities, on the one hand, recognized the existence of *mahalla*s but at the same time referred to them (in the *sijill*s, for example) as if they were *hara*s. In other words, Mahallat al-Yahud is strictly speaking not a *mahalla* but a *hara*.[6] Finally, how useful are our notions of urban grids oriented by sectarian divisions, when *dhimmi* and Muslim families in that city were often co-owners of residential properties both inside and outside traditional *dhimmi* neighborhoods?

This article contributes to the literature in three ways. First, by documenting the purchase and sale of residential properties among Christians and between them and Muslims and Jews, it offers a concrete picture of the general (and so far impressionistic) patterns of *dhimmi* residential distribution in Ottoman Damascus over a century-long period. In an effort to secure accuracy, the data are analyzed from different perspectives and with respect to various variables. Second, the article follows the recurring references to a number of Christian individuals who, together with their Muslim and Jewish associates, appear to have been particularly active on the residential market, and proposes a pattern of their activity. Most importantly, this study suggests the following: although the material in the *sijill* registers makes evident the role that religious affinity played in matters of residential choice and the shared tendency of Muslims, Christians, as well as Jews to seek both the real and imagined security of segregated urban space, the registers equally document the rather surprising fact that, for a variety of reasons, a certain number of Damascene Christians and Muslims not only crossed sectarian boundaries to inhabit the same public space of mixed neighborhoods, but went further to live side by side inside the private space of shared dwellings.

The Documentary Evidence

The material in this study is based on a total of 1,078 documents collected from 78 *sijill*s covering the century-long period under investigation.[7] Of this total, 705 documents involve Christians in residential purchase and sale transactions with other Christians, Muslims, or Jews. Furthermore, a total of 134 documents of the following types of transactions were used: *dhimmi* residential rentals from family (*ahli*) and charitable (*khayri*) Muslim and *dhimmi waqf*s; the establishment of Christian family and charitable *waqf*s on residential properties; *dhimmi waqf* trading in residential property; and loan transactions in which Christians used residential property as collateral (*bayʿ al-wafaʾ*). In addition, in order to gain a comparative perspective on Christian residential patterns, the following two sets of documents were also examined: all residential transactions involving Jews (93 in all)—among themselves and with Muslims and Christians that were recorded in the *sijill*s; and a total of 146 intra-Muslim residential transactions that were randomly chosen from 17 of the *sijill*s across the period under study.[8]

Until the mid-1860s when Ottoman Tanzimat measures involving the administration of justice took effect in Damascus, the *shariʿa* courts of that city, like those of many cities in the Empire, were the only official courts available to Muslim, Christian, and Jewish men and women. The courts dealt with a myriad of legal matters: they looked into lawsuits, officiated marriage and divorce contracts, divided up legacies, and acted as notaries of and depositaries for legal agreements and transactions. Because the courts possessed both the power of uncontested legal implementation and the capacity of secure registration, the vast majority of business deals, residential and otherwise, took place under their auspices.

The courts followed a consistent and highly formulaic format in documenting the purchase and sale of residential properties.[9] Most documents (*hujja*s) registered the following: the names of the men and women buying, selling, co-owning, and witnessing;[10] the kind and size of the residence[11] and the manner in which the seller had acquired it;[12] the quarter and *zuqaq* in which the property was located and the names of the neighbors (property owners, public institutions, or streets); the price involved; and the date of the transaction. It should be noted that many purchase and sale transactions involved more than a single buyer and/or seller but almost without exception each document involved only one single property. The sold properties were not, however, always whole residences, but shares thereof.[13]

Real estate transactions are businesslike, dry, and repetitive. As court documents, they fail to stir the moral imagination as documents on crimes are apt to do, for instance. Moreover, their strength is solely in numbers, in the patterns that a whole series of them enables us to establish. Every once in a while, however, a crack fractures the legal formulary and a glimpse is allowed into the private world of the men and women who were busily trading houses and changing addresses. For example, we do not really know much about the life of Ilyas w. Jirjis ʿAssaf of Damascus; we do not know whether he ever lived in a house he did not intend to sell. We do know, however, that in the 1780s he speculated on the real estate market, bought and sold at least two properties in the Jewish quarter, was involved in lengthy litigation with a Muslim man over one them, and made 300 *qurush* in profit from the other. He did not leave his children any property. His daughter, Warda, married Butrus w. Yusuf Maʿrufi and together they bought a house in Bab Musalla in Zuqaq al-Arbaʿin in August 1825. In July 1837, her brother Musa and his wife Lucia b. Butrus al-Miʿrawi moved to join them in Bab al-Musalla, purchasing a house in the same *zuqaq*. Another brother, Jubran, inherited from a cousin 7 1/4 *qirat*s of a substantial estate in Bab Sharqi which he sold in July 1835 for 2,000 *qurush*. After that the record is silent.[14] A shade more personal—and startling, given the *dhimmi*s' presumed insularity vis-à-vis Muslim society—is the case of Mariam b. Antun al-ʿAshshi, a Christian woman, who sought the Muslim court's assistance in evicting her mother from the house she owned (and was about to sell) despite her mother's anguished claim in court that her daughter had promised her lifelong shelter. The court complied.[15] Finally, there is the case of two Muslim women, Zeinab b. Muhammad al-Najjar and Amina b. Muhammad al-Zaghluli, who went to court in order to prevent a Jewish man from moving into their neighborhood—in the Jewish quarter, no less—lodging a suit against their Muslim neighbor, ʿAbd al-Ghani al-ʿAttar because he had leased him his house. Their quarrel with the legality of the lease centered on the well which, as a result of the lease, they would be obligated to share with the Jewish tenant. Interestingly, the defendant's winning response addressed the issue on the basis on which the plaintiffs had presented it, arguing for the validity of the lease based on the location of both houses and the well in the Jewish quarter, and providing documentary evidence as to their location.[16]

Christians in the Neighborhood

During the period under investigation the majority of the Damascene Christians purchased and rented residential properties in the Christian neighborhoods of the city.[17] The Christians purchased houses in 637 transactions, 73% (470) of which were located in the Christian quarter. On the rental market, 64% (45) of the 70 Christian tenants rented residences in the Christian areas of town.

These data need to be further delineated. First, the religious affiliation of the sellers is an important indicator of neighborhood distribution and must be noted: of the 637 Christian purchases, 78% (496) involved Christian sellers, 21% (133) Muslim sellers, and 1% (8) Jews. This delineation is significant for determining where the Christians lived because it could be argued that the preponderance of Christian sellers (to Christian buyers) over their Muslim and Jewish counterparts was a function of the existence of Christian neighborhoods. Can it be assumed that many, if not most, Christians actually lived in Maḥallat al-Naṣara simply because a high percentage of their residential purchases took place there? Or to state it differently, were Christian sellers simply trading in old homes and were buyers intent on living in their new houses, or were they, alternatively, playing the market, and either engaging in property speculation or buying houses they planned to lease out? Equally important in this regard is the Muslim seller of property located in the Christian quarter, and for the same reasons.

Christian property owners sold houses to other Christians 496 times, to Muslims 57 times, and to Jews 11 times. Of intra-Christian sales, 76% (379) were located in the Christian quarter, as compared with 64% (37) and 18% (2) when the buyers were Muslim and Jewish respectively. All in all, out of the 564 Christian properties sold, 74% (418) were located in the Christian quarter.

Of the 418 Christians engaged in selling property located in the Christian quarter, 235 had inherited the property and 63 had owned it for a considerable length of time. In other words, around 71% of the sellers were engaged in selling their own old homes. In addition, of these same 418 properties, 66% (277) had two, three, and sometimes four Christian neighbors. The fact that a considerable number of Christians were engaged in selling their homes should not be interpreted as a sign of Christian flight from the Christian quarter or from the city since, as already mentioned, the vast majority of the buyers were themselves also Christian. Moreover, because many of the sales were of shares of properties (as opposed to entire ones), many sellers continued to live in their (now smaller) residences.

As far as the buyers are concerned, to what extent can it be assumed that they were involved in buying homes as opposed to investments—that they were not intent on either remarketing the property or leasing it out for rental income? Unfortunately, the documents do not delve into the plans of the buyers or the eventual disposition of the property. However, we do know that among the buyers, 36% (136) already owned shares in those properties or were dealing with family members. In other words, over one third of the buyers already had some vested interest in the property or were expanding on their holdings. What about the rest? How many among them were intent on making the Christian quarter their home? The answer to this question is supplied not by the buyers themselves but from a twofold analysis involving residential rentals, on the one hand, and speculation in real estate and its distribution among different confessional groups, on the other.

A House to Let?

Like most properties in the city, the vast majority of Christian-purchased properties were not intended for rent. In Ottoman Damascus of the eighteenth and nineteenth centuries, much effort and capital were invested in home ownership and home rentals were few and far between. As noted by Abdel Nour and Marcus for eighteenth-century Aleppo and by Faroqhi for Ankara and Kayseri of a century earlier, home ownership was universally considered a form of financial security and a symbol of social status. Such an attitude was not only understandable given the insecurities of a fluctuating economy, but also translatable into reality because of the wide-ranging prices of homes in many Ottoman cities and the relative ease with which homes could be bought and sold.[18] All three authors have also noted for their respective cities what appears to be also true of Damascus: in contrast to the huge market in commercial and agricultural rental property, homes were rarely leased, or to put it differently, most people bought homes in order to live in them.[19]

This is borne out by the data. Of the total of 109 residential properties rented by *dhimmi*s, only 19% (21) were privately-owned residences and only 9% (10) were Christian-owned. Excluding the 18 *bayʿ al-wafaʾ* rentals, the remaining 70 residential rentals belonged to Muslim and Christian *waqf*s (42 and 11 respectively). Most of these *waqf*s were located in Maḥallat al-Naṣara; the rest were scattered in Kharab, Maydan, Qaymariyya, and Maḥallat al-Ya-hud.[20]

The records of the court comprise thousands of documents relating to *waqf*s, both Muslim and *dhimmi*. Among those a relatively small number concern *waqf* purchases of residential real estate. In the sample used for this study, there were only thirteen such documents pertaining to Christian *waqf*s. Eleven of those property purchases were located in the Christian quarter where their tenants were Christian. Although it is evident that the *waqf*s dominated the residential rental market, it is important to note that this market pales in comparison to commercial and agricultural rentals in which both the *waqf*s and private entrepreneurs were heavily invested.[21]

Buying to Sell

Although most men and women bought residential properties in order to make them their homes, a fairly large number of Damascenes acquired property neither for occupancy nor for leasing purposes, but as a way of making money. It has already been noted that the vast majority of sale transactions document the ownership history of the property at hand, listing properties either as inherited (and from whom) or bought (and at what date). It is thanks to this information as well as the fact that a buyer in one document will often appear as a seller in another, that we can more or less follow in the wake of certain men and women who were active on the real estate market. For instance, on 15 April 1787 a Christian man, Yusuf w. Shahin Sawaya, bought from Mikhail, Yusuf, and Helena w. ʿAbbud al-Hamawi and their mother, Mariam b. Mikhail al-Sabbagh, 16 *qirat*s of a house in Maḥallat al-Naṣara in Zuqaq al-Qasba for 600 *qurush*. On 25 May he sold that property to Musa w. Mikhail al-Dibaʿi for 650 *qurush*. In another instance, the capital gain was more impressive: On 12 August 1776 Musa w. Khadr, *shaykh al-ḥara al-yahudiyya,* bought from Muhammad b. Mustafa al-Halabi a house in the

Jewish quarter for 1,000 *qurush*. Two weeks later he sold the house to Ya'qub
w. Salmon al-Sarraf for 1,800 *qurush*. Apparently, the first Muslim owner
was speculating as well; he had bought the property three weeks before selling it.[22]

Some of these deals involved several parties and were quite complex: for
example, on 20 May 1806 Mikhail w. Antun al-Qarisati bought 2 1/6 *qirats*
of a house in Maḥallat al-Naṣara from Mikhail and Jubran w. Yusuf Srur for
800 *qurush*. Antun probably never set foot in his new home, for before he left
court that day he sold it to Musa w. Shehada al-Qazah for 830 *qurush*. For his
part, Musa went on to complete his purchase of the property, doing so in four
different transactions at the end of July. In the largest of those, he bought 11
qirats from Mariam b. Abraham and her minor children for 6,013 1/2 *qurush*.
On that same day he sold the entire house to the *qissis* (priest) Musa w. Jiryis
al-Himsi for 10,500.[23]

At times the buying and selling appear like a game of musical chairs.
For example, on 6 November 1797 Abraham w. Jirjis Salbin sold 12 *qirats*
of a house in Qaymariyya in equal shares each to Jubran w. Abraham Saba
al-Ba'li and Mariam b. Musa Shatila for 600 *qurush*. Abraham himself had
purchased the property from Mariam on two recent occasions. Mariam, who
had inherited 4 1/2 *qirats*, now had 10 1/2 and Jubran increased his share
from 6 to 12 *qirats*. The seller held on to 1 1/2 *qirats*. On the same day, Jirjis
w. Musa Muhanna bought 12 *qirats* of the same property from Jubran and
Mariam, leaving Mariam with 4 1/2, Jubran with 6, and Abraham with 1 1/2
qirats, respectively. The price he paid was 600 *qurush*. In the last transaction,
Jubran bought from Abraham and Mariam 2 *qirats* of the property for 100
qurush. At the end of it all, Jirjis owned 12 *qirats*, Jubran owned 8, Mariam
4, and Abraham nothing at all.[24]

As made evident by this series of transactions, cashing in on the residential real estate market often involved much more than simply buying a
property and then immediately placing it back on the market. At times shares
of the same property had to be bought from several co-owners, as a result
of which the seller found himself in a much stronger position to negotiate a
favorable price—having come up with a new package, so to speak. This is
apparently what Salmon w. Haim al-Hakham al-Sarraf did, for in July 1784
he sold to Salih Agha, for the price of 8,015 *qurush,* a property in the Jewish
quarter that he had bought in five different transactions spanning the previ-

ous five years.[25] At other times, the property was in fact given a facelift, as in the case of Mustafa b. Muhammad Halabi al-Dusuqi, who bought a house in Maḥallat al-Naṣara in two transactions in January and February 1871. He refurbished the house, adding a reception room on the second floor (qaṣr) and a stone stairwell, and resold the property for a hefty 2,400 qurush in June of that year.[26]

Reading the real estate transactions, it becomes clear that quick cash could be made by those diligent enough to keep a watchful eye on the market. For example, on 26 January 1807, ʿUthman Agha b. Muhammad bought from Khalil w. Mikhail Shalhub and his children Simʿan and Marwa 5 qiraṭs of a house in Bab Sharqi in Zuqaq al-Masbak for 50 qurush. The house was co-owned by Suleiman w. Jabbur (1 7/8 qiraṭs), who on that day bought from ʿUthman those 5 qiraṭs for 60 qurush. Clearly, it took some scheming to put together a deal in which a quick preemptive purchase yielded 10 qurush in a matter of minutes.[27]

The orchestration of speculators is often impressive. For example, in an interesting and complicated lawsuit dated 9 May 1781, two Jewish men, ʿId w. Yusuf Arazi and Yaʿqub w. Yusuf al-ʿAttar, appointed Salmon w. Haim as their wakil at noon and went to court where, through their wakil, they prevailed against Khadr w. Haim al-Sabban to sell them a property he had purchased that morning on the grounds that they, who were separate neighbors, had the right of preemption (shifaʿt al-jiwar). As a result, the two men paid Khadr the 1,300 qurush he had spent and acquired title to the property. On the following day, both men returned to court in order to sell that same property to Haim w. Shehada w. Haim al-Sarraf, Salmon's nephew, for 1,400 qurush.[28]

The record often makes evident that real estate transactions were not always about the business of buying and selling houses. The settling and/or masking of debts went hand in hand with speculative and financial deals, as is apparent from the following series of transactions involving several Christian and Muslim men and women: In July 1780, Abraham w. Mikhail al-ʿArqabji bought from his wife, Mariam, the Bab Sharqi house where she had lived for almost twenty years for 6,000 qurush. Several weeks later, on 15 August, he sold this property to Ibrahim b. ʿAbd al-Fattah for 8,550 qurush. Next day, the new owner sold this property to Musa al-Shammas and Helena b. Mikhail Shalhub for 3,820 qurush. In early September, Musa and Helena together sold the house to a Christian man, ʿAbd al-Ghani w. Yusuf al-Sabbagh, for 4,020 *qurush*. On the following day, ʿAbd al-Ghani met Musa and Helena in court and sold them the house back for 4,020 *qurush*. In January 1782 Musa bought Helena's 12 *qirat*s for 2,000 *qurush* and became sole owner of the property.[29]

Non-resident buyers/sellers complicate the history of neighborhoods and shed an interesting light on the possibilities of making money in the housing market. They also make clear that real estate was not where big money was made.[30]

The wheeling and dealing of these individuals also shed a light on the constituency of neighborhoods. A comparative analysis of their activities along religious lines and in different neighborhoods of the city is instructive.

In contrast to the 71% of the 418 Christian sellers who sold properties inside the Christian quarter that they had either inherited or owned for many years, 20% (82) of the sellers had owned the property for less than two years and were apparently engaged in speculation.[31] The fact that these Christian sellers were speculators obviously disqualifies them as real residents of Christian neighborhoods—in other words, their fleeting ownership in Christian neighborhoods had no effect on the sectarian constituency of these areas.[32] What is significant, on the other hand, is the identity of their clients—or more accurately, their victims: in 76 of the 82 speculation deals concluded in the Christian quarter, the buyer was Christian as well (the remaining six were all Muslims).[33] The number of Muslim property speculators in the Jewish and Christian areas of town was higher. Muslims sold a total of 173 properties to various *dhimmi* men and women, of which 124 properties were located in *dhimmi* areas and 48% (59) were only bought to sell. In the vast majority of cases this activity took place in the Christian quarter, and the property was promptly resold to a Christian party: of the 90 properties that Muslims sold to Christians in Maḥallat al-Naṣara, nearly 50% (43) had been bought a week or two earlier from other Christians. These Muslim sellers did not alter the Christian constituency of the quarter; they merely shuffled Christian ownership around.[34]

Interestingly, this pattern is much less evident in Muslim/*dhimmi* transactions outside the traditional *dhimmi* quarters, where only around 17% of Muslim sellers were engaged in speculation. These were areas in which Muslims also inherited many of the properties they eventually sold to Christians or Jews.[35]

Since Muslim property sales to *dhimmi* buyers are bound to be concentrated in *dhimmi* areas, comparing them to the sample of intra-Muslim sales is instructive. Out of a total of 146 properties sold, only 6% (9) of the residences were located in Maḥallat al-Naṣara, and only one of those was bought for resale. None of the 146 sales took place in the Jewish quarter. Overall, however, a total of 9% (13) of intra-Muslim purchases were intended for speculation.

Although it may be argued that a sample of 146 documents is hardly representative of the thousands of intra-Muslim residential transactions that we know were registered with the court, the sample is suggestive of a pattern of Muslim activity that appears to be quite different as far as the Christian and Jewish *mahalla*s were concerned. Whereas speculation in residential properties in *dhimmi* areas was certainly not limited to Muslims, and while many Muslim men and women inherited residences and lived in those areas, it is evident that Muslim buyers in those areas were more likely to be enterprising men and women than new arrivals next door. And even as this impressionistic comparison stands in need of further research, it does make it evident that neighborhood concentrations simply based on the identity of the buyers can be very misleading.

The fact that most Christian sellers traded in long-owned Christian property in the Christian quarter and sold to Christian buyers and that speculation deals—no matter who the speculator was—also placed properties in the Christian quarter in Christian hands—does all this mean that the Christian quarter was in fact solidly Christian?

Not all Muslim buyers in the Christian quarter were speculators. In fact, altogether, the purchase and sale transactions make reference to a Muslim neighbor in the Christian quarter 131 times. In addition, although we have no way of knowing how they disposed of their purchases, we cannot assume that all 55 Muslim buyers of homes in Maḥallat al-Naṣara were speculators in the making.[36]

Much more indicative of Muslim presence in the Christian areas is the ownership history of Muslim sellers. Of the 90 Muslim sellers dealing with Christians, 20 had inherited their properties and 17 others had owned their homes for a long period of time. All in all, only 41% of Muslim sellers (as compared to 71% of Christian sellers) were engaged in selling their old homes in the Christian quarter. Although mention of inherited and long-owned Muslim property in the Christian quarter represents strong evidence that at least some Muslims did indeed make that quarter their home, it is noteworthy that this evidence appears in transactions in which these same Muslims were engaged in selling their properties to Christians. In other words, they were either leaving those areas altogether (when selling whole residences) or diluting Muslim presence in them (when the sales were of partial properties).

Compared to Muslims, Jewish men and women were less actively engaged in the Christian housing market—they were altogether much less engaged with Christians in general. There were 53 Jewish/Muslim residential transactions, 40 intra-Jewish purchase-and-sales, and 19 Jewish/Christian deals. All in all, Jews bought only seven properties in the Christian quarter and sold five, three of which had been inherited or long-owned. Mention of Jewish neighbors in the Christian quarter reached only seven.[37] The Christian neighborhoods were clearly not extremely attractive to Jewish homeowners.[38]

Not all of the Christians in Damascus lived in Maḥallat al-Naṣara. Christians bought 64 homes in Maydan/Bab al-Musalla, 41 in Qaymariyya, 26 in Kharab, and 23 in Maḥallat al-Yahud, but Christian purchases outside Maḥallat al-Naṣara represented only 27% of Christian purchases altogether. Among Christian sellers of real estate outside the Christian areas, only 16% of them had inherited their property or had owned it for a long time.[39]

In this section the attempt has been made to examine the data on residential real estate from several perspectives in order to obtain as accurate a picture as possible of the residential patterns of the Christian population in Damascus. Although the scope of the data provided by the courts' registers is limited, the material reviewed in this section makes possible the following conclusions.

First, the vast majority of the Christian inhabitants of Damascus chose to live among their coreligionists in the Christian areas of Bab Tuma and Bab Sharqi. Although a number of them bought homes and settled outside their *mahalla*, it was mostly in Christian neighborhoods that they bought, inherited, and inhabited homes that, when sold, were most likely to be sold to other Christians.

Second, for many Damascenes of all religious persuasions, real estate offered a quick and relatively easy way to make money. The returns, it is true, were relatively modest, but the data suggest that the market was both open and dynamic. Furthermore, although speculation in real estate was by no means a Muslim monopoly, the evidence indicates that at least half of Muslim buyers of real estate in the Christian areas were likely to be speculators—that is to say, half of the Muslim buyers of homes in Maḥallat al-Naṣara were not in reality going to live in them. It also appears that most Muslim real estate speculation was centered on Christian buyers in the Christian areas.

Third, because the vast majority of intra-Christian purchases were in Maḥallat al-Naṣara, it is not surprising that this is where Christian speculators were most concentrated. What is surprising, however, is the high number of Christian speculators among Christian buyers. The combined concentration of Christian speculators and the relatively high presence of Muslim speculators in Christian neighborhoods must have both resulted from and generated a particularly competitive market. The preference of a growing Christian population to remain within the confines of its traditional neighborhoods may have been the cause. Regardless, it is equally evident that many Muslim buyers were salesmen and that from a methodological point of view, using the religious identity of buyers to reach conclusions regarding the constituency of neighborhoods—as is the case with some older *sijill*-based studies—is misleading.

Fourth, the conspicuous presence of Muslim speculators in Christian neighborhoods should not be allowed to obscure the fact that Muslims lived in those areas. There is no question that Muslims and Christians were often neighbors as well as partners in the business of real estate. Indeed, the material in the *sijill* suggests that many were also co-owners of the same residences.

Sharing Residential Space

Musa w. Shukri Shiha must have been an enterprising man. Shortly after Ibrahim al-Bunduqji died sometime in 1767, he bought from Katiba, the latter's daughter, her share of the house that al-Bunduqji had left for his many children. Katiba's share amounted to 2 3/4, 1/8, and 1/16 *qirats*—insignificant in itself, but important for the rest of al-Bunduqji's many other heirs. Musa Shiha promptly sold Katiba's share the day after he bought it to Musa and Hanna, Katiba's brothers. Ibrahim's three other daughters, Rahma, Mariam, and Khatun already owned through inheritance 8 3/4 and 1/2 *qirats* of the property. Fourteen years later, Musa and Hanna's wife, Taqla b. Ishaq al-Turk, bought from Khatun 3 *qirats* of the property. According to the document, Musa was already the owner of 10 and Taqla of 3 1/2 *qirats*—indicating that several deals had taken place since the initial transaction. Three years later, in 1783, Hanna and his wife Taqla purchased from Mariam b. ʿAbbud al-Naqqash, Musa's wife, 3 *qirats* of the property her husband had left her. By the end of 1783, Hanna and his wife had become sole owners of the house in its entirety. It was then that Hanna established a *waqf* on 10 *qirats* of the property. The *waqf* would benefit the poor from among the Jacobite Christians after his death.[40]

The history of this property is one of division and reconsolidation. It illustrates the divisive effect that Islamic law of inheritance brings to property and the continuous attempt on people's part to reconsolidate properties to render them either inhabitable or marketable. Islamic law, which the courts applied to legacies across sectarian lines, is complex. It recognizes a large number of possible heirs and lays down intricate rules as to who receives what, depending on gender as well as relationship to the deceased.[41] Although many properties were reconsolidated through intrafamilial sales, the existence of a large number of heirs often made the collective sale of the property to an outside buyer and the splitting of cash rather than *qirats* more convenient. This is illustrated by a case—albeit atypical—in which a total of 27 men sold a house they had collectively inherited. The house appears to have been of substantial size—it sold for 11,000 *qurush*—but clearly no house was large enough to accommodate that many men (and their families).[42] Alternatively, establishing a *waqf* was another means by which to maintain the integrity of the property and protect it from division.[43]

Divisive as they may have been as far as residential property is concerned, *shariʿa* laws of inheritance benefitted a large pool of men and women by giving them shares—albeit sometimes minuscule—in the residential market. Many chose to sell their shares, mostly to siblings eager to reconsolidate what the law had splintered. That so many real estate transactions involved relatives trading shares of the same property is testimony to this.[44]

The sale and purchase of shares of houses—as opposed to entire properties—dominated the real estate market, and relatively few houses sold in their entirety. Of the total of 944 properties traded between and among the different religious groups, only 34% (323) involved entire properties. The rest were sales of shares of houses that were sometimes smaller than one *qirat*.

At first glance, this does not appear surprising. Given the generational segmentation of property, very few individuals owned entire estates—unless reconsolidated through purchase. It is this factor that accounts for the high percentage (31%) of intrafamilial sales among intra-Christian residential deals.

However, the segmentation of residential properties and the active trade they generated were not brought about by inheritance laws alone. Although many among the buyers of partial residences were heirs to estates they were eager to reconsolidate or speculators who stood ready to cash in on their eagerness, a large number of the men and women who bought homes of a few *qirat*s belonged to neither group: they were simply buying affordable housing. In so doing, they often became co-owners with virtual strangers.

This state of affairs was not unique to Damascus. Abraham Marcus' work on eighteenth-century Aleppo reveals identical patterns. And as he rightly points out, in spite of the crowding and the loss of privacy involved in shared housing, partial ownership did indeed make it possible for a much wider segment of the urban population to own permanent and secure shelter. The less well-to-do among the Damascenes appear to have dealt with the situation in the same way as their fellow Ottomans in Aleppo: they used the *shari'a* court to segment residences in ways that made house-sharing both formal and reasonable.[45]

The segmentation of property took place in three ways, as reflected in the language of the transactions. First, and only rarely, one or more specific rooms (*masakin*)—the northern *murabba'* (quadrangle), for example—were designated for sale.[46] Second, occasionally a property was actually segmented—with sections carved out of the original house (*dar*) and transformed into smaller units (*muqassam*s). Although many of the transactions are short on details and simply describe the sectioned off area as such—"*al-muqassam al-mafruz (*or *al-maqsum) min al-dar*"—an occasional document will not only indicate the number of *qirat*s constitutive of the *muqassam*, but will also list the rooms included in the unit.[47]

Third, in most sale transfers either cost or architectural design gave rise to formal instead of actual dividing walls. In other words, a certain number of *qirat*s were bought and sold. At times a special note is added concerning either a certain share in, or simply the right to use, the courtyard (*saha*), the well (*bir*), and the door (*haq al-tawassul wa'l-istitraq*).[48]

Deciphering the spatial logic behind the legal segmentation of property is complicated by uncertainties regarding architectural vocabulary and its regional variations.[49] Furthermore, the *qirat* as the unit of measurement is useless for determining the size of the structures involved. Occasionally, however a detailed document is revealing, as in this instance where 3 1/7 *qirat*s of a house were sold. The house had two courtyards, each surrounded by a two-story structure of several rooms.[50] This property, which must originally have been two individual houses—as suggested in the latter part of the document, which refers to the "aforementioned two houses"—was clearly very large, which in turn indicates that the sold share of 3 1/7 *qirat*s was fairly significant. However, nothing in the document explains how the co-owners translated legally defined segments into their spatial equivalents or how they exercised their *qirat*-based rights in daily life. What does it mean, for example, to own 3 1/7 *qirat*s of a courtyard, a stairwell, a pool, or a latrine? If use was of the essence here, how did men and women trade in the currency of the *qirat* and what exactly did they trade it in for?[51]

The segmenting of residences had a parallel in the use of the *hawsh*. The *hawsh*—or collective housing—has been described at length by both Abdel Nour and Raymond. Defined simply as a group of modest residences surrounding a common courtyard, the *hawsh* was apparently an urbanized version of a rural type of building that came to accommodate the housing needs of the city poor—especially those among them who had just moved from the countryside. Raymond adds that the *hawsh* is but one of several types of collective dwellings to emerge in Ottoman (and pre-Ottoman) Middle Eastern cities—the caravanserai (*wakala, funduq, khan*, etc.) and the uniquely Egyptian *rab'* being others. These types of buildings served the residential needs of various kinds of people, both in transit (such as merchants) or permanently (such as the urban poor). What distinguishes the *hawsh* from other types is not merely that it was primarily housing for the poor—as opposed to temporary accommodation for merchants and their wholesale goods—but that it was the poor's collective compromise: a type that allowed several families access to a courtyard. Abdel Nour and Raymond both agree that the *hawsh* did not represent the "degradation of nobler forms." In other words, although the *hawsh* represented a form of collective living involving different families living around a common courtyard, it was modeled on rural forms and hence was, in origin if not in function, different from the shared houses that had once seen better days and single owners.[52]

Origins notwithstanding, what is remarkable about the *hawsh* is the way it served the needs of the urban population in the same way as the segmented and shared residences: it made possible affordable housing with access to a courtyard. Abdel Nour and Raymond's insistence that the noble Arab house of old did not simply degenerate into the *hawsh* should not obscure the fact that many such houses were "degraded" nonetheless and that for a large number of people the sections of "degraded" wholes were home.[53]

Among the records examined for this study, there are 28 separate references to a *hawsh*. Well into the 1890s, all the *hawsh*s referred to were located in the Jewish quarter and most of their inhabitants were Jews. Mention is made in nineteenth-century documents of *hawsh*s in Bab Sharqi, Kharab, and Maydan where many *dhimmi*s lived, but the number of Jewish buyers remains high, suggesting the relative poverty of the Jewish community—especially when compared to its situation in the eighteenth century.[54]

It is evident that a large number of the inhabitants of Damascus lived in segmented housing—both inherited and purchased. This was true of Muslims, Christians, and Jews. Seventy-six percent (377 out of 496) of intra-Christian sales and purchases and 62% (91 out of 164) of intra-Muslim deals involved shares of homes. Across sectarian lines, the affordability of such housing accounted for these high percentages as much as inheritance and—to a lesser extent—speculation.

It should come as no surprise that the ratio of partial to entire sales dropped noticeably in intercommunal sales. Fifty-one percent (96 out of 190) of Christian/Muslim sales were of shares. A similar pattern is noted for Jewish transactions in which 58% (23 out of 40) of intra-Jewish sales were of shares, compared to 47% (25 out of 53) of Jewish-Muslim transactions. In other words, buyers and sellers belonging to the same religious group tended to trade in shares more frequently than those who crossed religious divides.[55]

These figures raise two important points. On the one hand, while intra-familial sales go a long way toward explaining the preponderance of partial sales in intercommunal transactions, it is also evident that when the Damascenes bought and sold real estate, the preference was to share properties with coreligionists and to buy entire lots rather than shares when crossing religious lines. This is not, of course, surprising. However, it is also evident that a great number of shared housing was traded across sectarian lines—purchases that were neither intrafamilial nor speculative. Altogether, Muslims and Christians traded a total of 96 partial properties, of which 31% (30) involved speculation and 51% (49) had been inherited or long-owned. Most of the shared properties were in Maḥallat al-Naṣara.[56]

But if men, women, and entire families adapted the single-family Arab house and the rural *ḥawsh* to the immediate and pressing demands of city life and moved in with strangers across the courtyard, how far did this accommodation go? Did intracommunal co-ownership translate into cohabitation? Given that most people actually lived in the houses they bought, it appears that many Damascenes—Muslims, Christians, and, to a lesser extent Jews—in fact came to be co-owners of residential properties in sufficiently conspicuous numbers, ignored or suspended sectarian differences, and allowed themselves to share the private space of home.

The figures and considerations described above evoke realities starkly at odds both with the image of the single-family Arab house and with the relatively high degree of neighborhood insularity already described. Blind to religious identity, poverty and need brokered the parcelization of properties and the crowding of space. They also added complications to daily life—the sacrifice of privacy, for example—so well described by Marcus.[57] In addition, it appears that the confluence of poverty on the one hand, and the wish to remain in Christian areas on the other, made possible the crossing of communal divides in unexpected ways. We know very little about the Christian and Muslim families who shared the courtyards and facilities of segmented housing.[58] We can guess that, given the choice, most would have preferred the communal insularity of neighborhood and home. We cannot, therefore, marvel at their open-mindedness or conclude that sectarian divisions were nonexistent—the events of July 1860, when thousands of inner-city Christians were massacred and their quarters burnt, belie such thinking. All we can do is note the facts of their shared daily lives, and agree with Abdel Nour's statement that "Si, à l'image d'une société cloisonnée, les batiments de la ville arabe reproduissent à l'infini le repleiment des groupes familiaux, ils ne sont nullement à l'abri des contingences du monde."[59]

Conclusion

In this article the attempt was made to study the residential patterns of the Christians of Damascus over a century-long period. The registers that constitute the primary sources for this study are abundant in number but limited in scope. They supply the basic market "facts," describe the residential structures, their rooms, courtyards, and occasional gardens, but leave to the socio-historic imagination the use to which these structures were put—in other words, they do not, cannot by their nature, speak of the living that daily transformed architectural structures and the market shares they represented into homes.[60]

The material gleaned from these *sijill*s indicates that the Christian population of Damascus was more cloistered in Maḥallat al-Naṣara than suggested both by earlier studies and in comparison to other cities such as Aleppo. Contrary to Abdel Nour's somewhat tentative remarks, however, this phenomenon was not a mid-nineteenth-century development. The data show a remarkable continuity from the eighteenth century in terms of both the location and the kind of residences purchased by the Christians. The reassessment of the constituency of Christian *maḥalla*s is in part based on a closer analysis of Muslim purchases—the fact that many of them were involved in speculation and therefore hardly participants in changing the sectarian character of Christian areas.

However, neither the preponderance of Christians in Maḥallat al-Naṣara nor the activities of Muslim speculators should obscure the presence of Muslim residents in these areas, among whom many also shared residences with Christians. Although such choices may have been engendered by poverty alone, they do invite us to reassess our notions, not of the existence of sectarian divides, but of the way in which such divides played themselves out in daily life.

The material presented is also suggestive of a relationship between the Christians' preponderance in Maḥallat al-Naṣara and their seeming willingness to share domestic space with Muslim families. In other words, if poverty drove Muslim families into intercommunal sharing of domestic space, the fact that the vast majority of these shared homes were located in Maḥallat al-Naṣara suggests that, as far as Christian families were concerned, the choice was dictated not only by poverty, but by the desire to remain in the Christian *maḥalla*.

That the drive for sectarian insularity and isolation should lead to the breakdown of intercommunal boundaries in the most sequestered of places—the home—is somewhat surprising. Paradoxical as it may appear to be, it nonetheless points to an important connection between the organization of domestic space, on the one hand, and the larger organization of urban quarters, on the other. This suggestion stands in need of further research, but is supported by the remarkable thematic parallels that separately cut across the literature on the "Muslim house," on the one hand, and the "Muslim city," on the other.[61]

Appendix

The following is a list of the *sijill*s, their dates, and, when known, the names
of their courts of origin. A substantial part of this research was carried out
at the University of Jordan's Markaz al-Wath'iq wa'l-Makhtutat, where the
Center keeps microfilm copies of a large number of Damascus *sijill*s. The
*sijill*s of the Center are, therefore, also followed by the appropriate microfilm
catalogue number. Page and case numbers were not always legible. Two Damascus microfilms are erroneously catalogued as Aleppo materials. Although
several of the later *sijill*s cover the period during and following the events of
July 1860, all the documents used in this paper predate these events.

Sijill Volume	Dates	Name of Court
sijill 123/film 222	1784–85	Unknown
sijill 173/film 209	1766	Unknown
sijill 174/film 209	1765–66	Unknown
sijill 199	1775–78	al-Kubra
sijill 201	1776–78	Qassam ʿAskari
sijill 204	1777–78	Qassam ʿArabi
sijill 210/film 209	1779–80	Unknown
sijill 211/film 225	1780	Unknown
sijill 212/film 225	1780–81	al-Baladiyya
sijill 213/film 225	1780–81	Unknown
sijill 214/film 225	1780–81	Unknown
sijill 216/film 225	1782–83	Unknown
sijill 217/film 193	1782–84	Unknown
sijill 218/film 193	1784–91	Unknown
sijill 219/film 193	1784–85	Unknown
sijill 220/film 193	1785–88	al-Kubra
sijill 239	1795–96	al-Kubra
sijill 240	1796–1801	Unknown
sijill 244	1800	Unknown
sijill 245	1799–1802	al-ʿAwniyya
sijill 247	1800	Unknown
sijill 250	1801–1802	Unknown
sijill 257	1806–1807	al-Kubra
sijill 267	1808–13	Qassam ʿArabi
sijill 269	1809–10	Unknown
sijill 270	1810	Unknown
sijill 271	1810–11	Unknown
sijill 272	1810–11	Unknown
sijill 275	1812–13	al-Kubra
sijill 283	1815	al-ʿAwniyya
sijill 297/Aleppo 114	1820–21	al-Maydan

Sijill Volume	Dates	Name of Court
sijill 298/Aleppo 114	1820–21	al-Kubra
sijill 300/film 191	1821–22	Unknown
sijill 301	1822–24	al-Bab
sijill 307	1825–26	al-Maydan
sijill 321	1830–31	Unknown
sijill 322	1830–31	al-Bab
sijill 323/film 201	1831–32	Unknown
sijill 326/film 201	1831–33	Unknown
sijill 327	1831–33	Qassam ʿArabi
sijill 336	1834–35	Unknown
sijill 346	1836–37	al-Bab
sijill 354	1838–39	Unknown
sijill 355	1838	Unknown
sijill 356	1838–39	Unknown
sijill 359	1839–40	Unknown
sijill 360	1840	Unknown
sijill 366/film 201	1841	al-Kubra
sijill 367/film 201	1841–42	Unknown
sijill 368/film 200	1839–41	Unknown
sijill 369/film 200	1842	al-Kubra
sijill 386	1844	al-Bab
sijill 389	1845–46	al-Bab
sijill 392	1846–47	al-Maydan
sijill 398	1847–48	al-Kubra
sijill 400	1847–48	Unknown
sijill 410	1848	Buzuriyya
sijill 411	1848–49	al-Maydan
sijill 417	1849	al-Kubra
sijill 421	1850	al-Kubra
sijill 426	1850–51	al-Maydan
sijill 466/film 200	1854	Unknown
sijill 467/film 200	1854	al-ʿAwniyya
sijill 470	1854–56	Unknown
sijill 475	1854–56	Sinaniyya
sijill 479/film 216	1855	al-Kubra
sijill 490	1856–58	Unknown
sijill 508	1860	Unknown
sijill 509	1860–61	al-Bab
sijill 511/film 205	1860–62	al-ʿAwniyya
sijill 516/film 205	1858–60	al-ʿAwniyya
sijill 517/film 205	1858–60	Qassam ʿArabi
sijill 520/film 205	1860–61	Sinaniyya
sijill 521/film 205	1859–61	al-Maydan
sijill 522/film 221	1859–61	al-Kubra
sijill 523/film 221	1859–61	al-Maydan
sijill 524/film 221	1860–62	al-Maydan
sijill 707/film 217	1784–87	Qassam ʿArabi

Notes

1. *Sijill* 212 (film 225)/Shawwal 1195.

2. See the appendix for the list of *sijill*s consulted.

3. See, for example, Suraiya Faroqhi, *Men of Modest Substance: House Owners and House Property in Seventeenth-Century Ankara and Kayseri* (Cambridge: Cambridge University Press, 1987); Andre Raymond, *The Great Arab Cities in the 16th–18th Centuries: An Introduction* (New York: New York University Press, 1984); Daniel J. Schroeter, "Jewish Quarters in the Arab-Islamic Cities of the Ottoman Empire," in *The Jews of the Ottoman Empire*, ed. with an introduction by Avigdor Levy (Princeton: Darwin Press, 1994). For studies on Syrian cities see, for example, Abraham Marcus, "Men, Women, and Property: Dealers in Real Estate in Eighteenth-Century Aleppo," *Journal of the Social and Economic History of the Orient* 26 (1983): 137–63; Marcus, "Privacy in Eighteenth-Century Aleppo: The Limits of Cultural Ideals," *International Journal of Middle Eastern Studies* 18 (1986): 165–83; Abdul-Karim Rafeq, "al-Bunya al-ijtimaʿiyya waʾl-iqtiṣadiyya li-Maḥallat Bab al-Musalla (al-May-dan) bi-Dimashq (1825–1875)," *Dirasat Tarikhiyya* 25/26 (March–June 1987): 7–62; Rafeq, *Ghazza: Dirasa ʿumraniyya wa-ijtimaʿiyya wa-iqtiṣadiyya min khilal al-wathʾiq al-sharʿiyya, 1857–1861* (Amman, Jordan: University of Jordan Press, 1980); Amnon Cohen, *Jewish Life under Islam: Jerusalem in the Sixteenth Century* (Cambridge: Harvard University Press, 1984); Antoine Abdel Nour, *Introduction à l'histoire urbaine de la Syrie Ottomane, 15–17 siècle* (Beirut: Lebanese University, 1982).

4. For example, certain properties are said to be located in *Maḥallat al-Naṣara bi-Zuqaq al-Zeitun tabiʿ Maḥallat al-Yahud.*

5. Abdel Nour, *Introduction*, 158–60. Abdel Nour's *athman*, based on a nineteenth-century source, consisted of Maydan, Qanawat, Suq Saruja, Salihiyya, ʿAmara, Qaymariyya, Nasara, and Shaghur. Compare to Abdul Aziz Azmeh, *Mirʾat al-Sham* (London: Riad El-Rayyes Books, 1987), 45–53, which lists two Maydans (upper and lower) and places both the Christian and Jewish quarters in Qaymariyya.

6. See Abdel Nour, "Types architecturaux et vocabulaire de l'abitat en Syrie aux XVIe et XVIIe siècle," in *L'Espace social de la ville Arabe*, ed. Dominique Chevallier (Paris: G.-P. Maisonneuve et Larose, 1979), 61, where the author argues against the notion that the semantic "anarchy" of these terms corresponds to the actual anarchy of the "Arab city" and suggests that the difference between *ḥara* and *ḥay* is that the first refers to a spatio-social entity, while the latter is purely spatial. In the *sijill*s consulted for this study, "*maḥalla*" is used consistently. The property is described as located in a certain *maḥalla* and a certain *zuqaq*. The term *ḥara* appears only in references to *shaykh al-ḥara.* In-

terestingly, the *sijill*s occasionally refer to a property as located in *Maḥallat al-Maydan in Maḥallat Bab al-Musalla*. This is explained in Abdul-Karim Rafeq, "al-Bunya al-ijtimaʿiyya," 9, where the author notes that Bab al-Musalla is the only *maḥalla* in the Maydan—which properly speaking is not a *maḥalla* but a *thumn* of the city.

7. The relative scarcity of *dhimmi* documents and the haphazardness of their distribution in the *sijill* both render the periodic sampling of the registers most unproductive. Instead, this researcher consulted a large number of volumes and analyzed all the *dhimmi* documents therein.

8. The following is the breakdown of the documents by type: 496 intra-Christian purchase and sale (P/S) transactions; 190 Christian-Muslim P/S; 19 Christian-Jewish P/S; 40 intra-Jewish P/S; 53 Jewish-Muslim P/S; 146 intra-Muslim P/S; 70 cases of Christians renting residential properties from Muslim and Christian *waqf*s; 21 cases of Christians renting privately-owned residences; 12 cases of Christians establishing *waqf*s on residential properties; 13 cases of charitable *waqf*s' P/S of residential properties; and 18 cases of *dhimmi* residential P/S due to the expiration of time specified on loans using residences as collateral. Excluded from the list are commercial purchase and sale transactions as well rental transactions and deals involving parcels of land both rural and urban.

9. For a particularly helpful description of *sijill* transactions, see James A. Reilly, "*Shariʿa* Court Registers and Land Tenure around Nineteenth-Century Damascus," *MESA Bulletin* 21 (1987): 155–69. Although Reilly's focus is on rural landed properties, which were dealt with differently by the court, most of what he describes for land transactions was also true of urban residential properties.

10. Minors, women, and individuals of status were often represented by others—*waṣi*s and *wakil*s. The scribes of the court primarily identified men and women by reference to the father's name, although less commonly available family names—many derived from place of origin or occupation—were also used. In addition, the scribes used a variety of linguistic and orthographic means to mark the religious affiliation of *dhimmi* parties. Typically, a Muslim man is listed as "Muhammad *ibn* (son of) Mustafa," a Muslim woman as "Fatima *bint* Ahmad," whereas a Christian man is listed as *al-madʿu* or *al-khawaja* (both dhimmi-specific titles) Mikhail *walad* ("dhimmified" son of) Bulus *al-dhimmi al-naṣarani* (the Christian); a Jewish woman as *al-madʿuwwa* Qamar *bint* Abraham *al-dhimmiyya al-yahudiyya* (the Jew). During most of the period under study, many *dhimmi* men's names were also purposely misspelled. These markers make documents pertaining to *dhimmi*s exceptionally easy to identify. Christian sects were not identified.

11. The actual dimensions of traded residences were never specified. Instead, the homes were measured in *qirat*s, with a whole constituting a total of 24 *qirat*s. The purchase and sale agreements more often than not traded in parts of resi-

dences, also measured in *qirats*. The number of *qirats* bought and sold could be anywhere from 23 *qirats* to a singe *qirat*. Additionally, fractions of *qirats* were not uncommon. Many sales listed portions of residences as, for example, 5 1/3, 1/8, and 1/16 *qirats*. The fractions themselves were never added up. In addition to the listed price, however, many documents included detailed descriptions of the properties, thus enabling the reader to gauge the relative size and luxuriousness of the establishment at hand.

12. For inherited properties, the name(s) of the most recent owner(s) and their relationship to the seller were documented; for purchased properties, the date of the purchase was usually, but not always, supplied. Occasionally, the scribes simply noted that the property had been "purchased earlier." On rare occasions, the name of the previous owner was noted. As will become evident, these data are most important for tracing the social lives of residences and the religious configuration of neighborhoods.

13. Of the 1,078 transactions reviewed, only three dealt with multiple properties — the sale of two separate residences in one; the sale of a house as well as part of another next door; and the simultaneous sale of a house and a shop.

14. *Sijill* 211 (film 225)/Ramadan 1195; *sijill* 218 (film 193)/Rabi' I 1205; *sijill* 220 (film 193)/Rabi' I 1201; *sijill* 307/end of dhu'l-Hijja 1240; *sijill* 336/Rabi' II 1253; *sijill* 346, 5 Rabi' I 1253.

15. *Sijill* 123/pp. 433–34/# 222/11 dhu'l-Qa'da 1200.

16. *Sijill* 298 (film Aleppo 114)/10 Jumada II 1237. It is noteworthy that this kind of argument, which speaks of social rather than of legal bias, was not repeated elsewhere in the *sijill*, despite the mixed residential character of many neighborhoods in Damascus. Whatever the grounds were on which the prejudicial claim was based — whether custom or sheer bias — the court did not show any interest in contesting its validity. Although it clearly aligned itself with the soundness of the defendant's response — which by implication suggests acceptance of the validity of the plaintiffs' objections, the court's ruling was based on considerations attaching to the validity of the documentary proof. See *sijill* 300 (film 191)/p. 41/3 dhu'l-Qa'da 1237 for a case in which a Jewish man leased a house from a Muslim family in the Jewish quarter and in which the issue of the well bore no mention.

17. The *sijill* employed the term "*mahalla*," more often than not when referring to the area in question such as "Mahallat al-Naṣara." On other occasions, the more specific references to "Bab Sharqi" or "Bab Tuma" were used.

18. Abdel Nour, *Introduction*, 109–10; Abraham Marcus, *The Middle East on the Eve of Modernity: Aleppo in the Eighteenth Century* (New York: Columbia University Press, 1989), 189–90; Marcus, "Men, Women, and Property," 138–39; Faroqhi, *Men of Modest Substance*, .

19. In *Men of Modest Substance*, 19, Faroqhi notes that in the *sijill*s of Ankara and

Kayseri individuals were identified by reference to the city quarter in which they resided, thus enabling the researcher to determine whether a seller owned two houses, at least in cases where the seller resided in a quarter other than the one in which the sold property was located (although she does not comment on the fact that, theoretically, owners of two houses in the same quarter would go unnoticed). This, unfortunately, was true of the Damascus *sijill* only as of the early 1860s; documents of the earlier period routinely identified individuals using their address, so to speak, only when they were villagers. The relative scarcity of rental transactions in the *sijill* cannot, I believe, be explained away by reference to out-of-court agreements. In a society where going to court was part of daily life, it is not reasonable to think that in this one instance the Damascenes, like their fellow Ottomans in Aleppo or Ankara, simply chose not to do so. See James A. Reilly, "Women in the Economic Life of Late-Ottoman Damascus," *Arabica* t. 42 (1995): 82.

20. The following is a detailed breakdown of the data on rentals: of the 109 *dhimmi* rentals, 70 (64%) properties were owned by *waqf*s (54 Muslim and 16 Christian family and charitable *waqf*s); 18 properties were *bayʿ al-wafa* rentals (involving 14 Christian debtors and ten Christian creditors), and 21 were private property (11 Muslim-owned, 10 Christian). Of this last group, of 21 tenants, 17 were Christian and 4 were Jewish. Ten of the 17 Christian tenants rented from Muslims and 7 from other Christians; all four Jewish tenants rented Muslim property.

21. Several of the *waqf* rentals were subleased and a large number involved agreements whereby the tenant invested in repairing the property in exchange for rent. See, for example, *sijill* 199/pp. 113–14/# 393/14 Shaʿban 1190 (*waqf* of the Mariamiyya Church in Maḥallat al-Naṣara); *sijill* 217 (film 193)/Muharram 1199 (*waqf* Muhammad al-Qattan in the Jewish Quarter); *sijill* 240/dhu'l-Hijja 1211 (*waqf* of the Ummayad Mosque in Kharab); and *sijill* 269/pp. 114–15/# 159 (Saidnaya *waqf*). For a useful description of the *waqf*, see Bahaeddin Yediyiliz, *Institution du vaqf au 18 siècle en Turquie: Étude socio-historique* (Ankara: Ministere de la Culture, 1990).

22. *Sijill* 220 (film 193)/8 Rajab 1201 and 18 Shaʿban 1201; *sijill* 199/end of Jumada II 1190 and 15 Rajab 1190. See also the case of ʿAli b. Khalil Banin (?) who bought from five Jewish brothers, their mother, and their aunt a house in Maḥallat al-Yahud for 3,200 *qurush*. Two weeks later he sold the property to Shehada w. Nasim Hassun for 3,252 *qurush* [*sijill* 220 (film 193)/12 Safar and 1 Rabiʿ I 1202].

23. *Sijill* 257/2 Rabiʿ I 1221; (2 documents); 12 and 13 Jumada I 1221 (four documents).

24. *Sijill* 240/p. 496/# 784; p. 496/# 785; p. 498/# 789. All are dated 15 Jumada I 1212.

25. *Sijill* 217 (film 193)/17 Ramadan 1199. Salmon w. Haim was, it seems, a veteran speculator in real estate. On 20 and 31 August 1780 he bought two adjacent properties located in Maḥallat al-Naṣara from their separate Christian and Muslim owners for 205 and 8,000 *qurush* respectively. On 31 August he sold them together to Muhammad b. Hassan al-Halabi for 8,760 *qurush* [*sijill* 210 (film 209)/Shaʿban 1194 and 1 Ramadan 1194].

26. *Sijill* 211 (film 225)/Rajab, 1195.

27. *Sijill* 257/16 dhu'l-Qaʿda 1221. See also *sijill* 257/6 dhu'l-Hijja, where Mustafa b. Muhammad al-Dirani bought 9 *qiraṭ*s of a property in Maḥallat al-Naṣara and sold it the same day to a co-owner.

28. *Sijill* 211 (film 225)/14 Jumada I 1195 and 15 Jumada I 1195.

29. *Sijill* 210 (film 209)/Rajab 1194/*Sijill* 210 (film 209)/13 and 14 Shaʿban 1194; *sijill* 210 (film 209)/13 and 14 Ramadan 1194; *sijill* 214 (film 225)/3 Safar 1196. See also *sijill* 250/four documents dated 18 Muharram 1217 and two documents dated 19 dhu'l-Qaʿda 1217 and end of dhu'l-Hijja 1217 for the following sequence of transactions: on 22 May 1802, a Christian man sold 5 1/4 *qiraṭ*s of a house to a Muslim buyer for 100 *qurush*. On March 15 of the following year, the original Christian owner bought back his house for 100 *qurush* and then immediately resold it to a different Muslim man for 130 *qurush*. On 25 April of the same year, the new Muslim owner resold the house to its original Christian owner for 160 *qurush*. The complexity of legal fiction and masking of debts and interest that appear to be involved in this series of transactions is not duplicated too often in the record. Instead, what one does come across often enough are two (usually consecutive) transactions in which a property is bought and immediately sold back to its original owner for the same price. See, for example, *sijill* 220 (film 193)/Rabiʿ I 1201; *sijill* 218 (film 193)/16 Shaʿban 1201; *sijill* 240/15 Jumada I 1212; *sijill* 257/6 dhu'l-Hijja 1221.

30. See Marcus, *Middle East*, 191–93. See also Nelly Hanna, *Making Big Money in 1600: The Life and Times of Ismaʿil Abu Taqiyya, Egyptian Merchant* (Syracuse: Syracuse University Press, 1998), for a *sijill*-based chronicle of a life in which fabulous riches were made.

31. From the methodological point of view, it is important to note that short-term ownership by itself should not necessarily signal speculation. A sudden need for cash triggered by an economic crisis must have led many new homeowners to sell. The assumption is made here, however, that it is unlikely that such a crisis would have taken place a day or a week after purchase. In many other cases, there exists documentary evidence showing that properties were resold for a quick profit. Compare with Abdel Nour, *Introduction*, 121, who expresses shock at the rapidity with which a house in Aleppo was sold in the 18th century—twelve years after its owner had bought it.

32. Christian enterprise outside the Christian quarter was not as ambitious. A total

of 146 properties were sold by Christians to Christians and other parties in the quarters of Maydan (52), Qaymariyya (36), Kharab (26), and Yahud (19). Out of this total only 18 (12%) properties had clearly been bought only for purposes of resale—almost all of them being located in Maydan and Qaymariyya.

33. Jewish buying patterns were significantly similar: out of a total of 61 properties sold by Jews, 12 (20%) had clearly been bought not for occupancy, but for resale. Eleven out of the 12 were located in the Jewish quarter, and nine properties were more or less immediately resold to Jewish buyers.

34. A similar pattern is evident in Muslim/Jewish transactions: 12 of the 25 properties sold by Muslims to Jews in the Jewish quarter and 3 of the 4 properties sold by Muslims to Christians in the Jewish quarter had been recently purchased.

35. Only 2 out of the 10 Qaymariyya sales, 3 out of 9 Kharab sales, and 2 of 21 Maydan sales of Muslims to Christians appear to have involved speculation.

36. Noteworthy is the fact that 37 of those 55 Muslim buyers bought their property from Christians.

37. Among the neighbors was the *hakham* [*sijill* 210 (film 209)/13 Safar 1195].

38. All in all, Jews bought 91 and sold 61 homes. As buyers, the Jews bought 70 (77%) of their homes in Maḥallat al-Yahud (8 in Nasara, 12 in Kharab, and one in Suq Saruja). As sellers, they also appear focused on their quarter, with 54 of the 61 homes (88%) sold located in the Maḥallat al-Yahud (of the rest, 5 were located in Nasara and 2 in Kharab). Thirty-seven of the 54 Jewish-owned homes in the Jewish quarter about to be sold had been inherited or long owned by their sellers (sales of Jewish inherited or long-owned property outside the Jewish quarter included only 3 in Nasara and 2 in Kharab). Looking at the overall picture of property transactions in the Jewish quarter, the subsidiary role of the Christians both as buyers and sellers becomes clear: 97 properties in the Jewish quarter switched owners; in 84 (87%) of those Jews were involved as either buyers or sellers and 39 (40%) times in both capacities. Muslims bought 7 properties and sold 25 in the Jewish quarter, while Christians bought 19 and sold 19 properties in the Jewish quarter. Of the Muslim sellers in the Jewish quarter, 9 had inherited their property, while 14 of the 19 Christian sellers had inherited theirs. Fourteen homes in the Jewish quarter had Muslim neighbors but only three had Christian neighbors, although, interestingly, the Catholic patriarch was among them [*sijill* 521 (film 205)/Shaʻban 1276]. Jewish tenants numbered 18 in all. The tenants were distributed in the following locations: Yahud (7), Kharab (8), and Nasara (3).

39. The following is the breakdown for inherited/long-owned Christian property: 36 in Maydan/Bab al-Musalla, 20 in Qaymariyya, 16 in Kharab, and 14 in Yahud. Christian presence in other areas of town is negligible. Only a handful of purchases took place in assorted areas such as Sinaniyya, Shaghur, and Salihiyya.

40. *Sijill* 173 (film 209), Shaʿban 1180; *sijill* 210 (film 209), Shawwal 1194; *sijill* 216 (film 225), Rajab and Shawwal 1197.

41. See, for example, the lawsuit instigated by a Jewish woman, Ghazala Aslan, against her two nephews by marriage who she claimed had fraudulently taken some of her possessions by misrepresenting *shariʿa* law and claiming that they were heirs to her deceased son (*sijill* 707 [film 217]/Jumada II 1197). It was apparently not uncommon for some *dhimmi*s to misrepresent either the law or their own family relationships in fraudulent attempts to inherit from others. See, for example, the case of the Christian man who took a Christian woman to court in an attempt to get a share of her inheritance from her deceased father, who he claimed was his cousin (*sijill* 508/p. 18/# 30/14 Shawwal 1276). For an illustration of *shariʿa* inheritance laws at work, see the case of Taqla, who, shortly after she had been widowed, sold her brother Ibrahim part of a house in Maḥallat al-Naṣara. The rest of the property belonged to Taqla's four daughters and their paternal uncle Simʿan w. Jirjis Qazma. The property had been inherited by Taqla, her daughters, and her brother-in-law from Taqla's husband Hanna w. Jirjis Qazma. In this case the paternal uncle was heir because Taqla had no sons [*sijill* 211 (film 225)/10 Rabiʿ I 1195].

42. *Sijill* 470/Jumada I 1271. For another example, see *sijill* 517 (film 205)/Jumada I 1277 for a transaction in which Mikhail Mishaqa bought a house for 13,000 *qurush* in Qaymariyya from five members of the extended Halbawi family—there were brothers, cousins, and uncles involved—and *sijill* 298 (Aleppo 214) for a case in which the eight heirs to Yusuf Shiha opted to sell the 12 *qiraṭs* he left them to Mariam b. Bulus, a Christian woman.

43. For examples of *waqf*s established by Christian and Jewish men and women on residential properties, see *sijill* 250/dhuʾl-Qaʿda 1216, in which a Christian woman converted 12 *qiraṭs* of a house in Bab Tuma into a charitable *waqf*, the beneficiaries in this instance being the poor Christians living in the Mariamiyya Church in Saidnaya (a town near Damascus). For other examples of charitable *waqf*s, see *sijill* 247/Shaʿban 1217 (beneficiary: the Maronite church); *sijill* 322/Safar 1247 (beneficiary: the Armenian *taʾifa* in Kisrwan). Other residential *waqf*s specified the owner as beneficiary until his/her own death, at which point the *waqf* became a charitable *waqf*. For example, in *sijill* 216 (film 225)/Rajab 1197 a Christian man established a *waqf* on 10 *qiraṭs* of a house in Bab Sharqi, made himself beneficiary during his lifetime and the poor among the Jacobite Christians after his death.

44. One hundred fifty-three out of 496 (31%) of intra-Christian properties bought and sold involved the reconsolidation of split property—most among family members.

45. See Marcus, "Men, Women, and Property," and Abdel Nour, *Introduction*, 118ff.

46. *Sijill* 210 (film 209)/15 Muharram 1195, for example, involved the sale of two *murabba‘*s, a small room (*oda*), a kitchen, and a reception area. In addition, use of the door, courtyard, latrine, and well (*bir*) were included.

47. *Sijill* 199/pp. 126–27/# 410/Sha‘ban 1190 involved the sale of a *muqassam* that comprised an *oda*, a *murabba‘*, a kitchen, and two *qasr*s.

48. Some sales involved a combination of these types of segmentation which resulted in even smaller shares, such as the sale in one document of 10 *qirat*s of a *qasr* that had just been added to the property [*sijill* 210 (film 209)/18 Rabi‘ I 1195].

49. See Abdel Nour, "Types architecturaux," where he addresses this specific question. In *Introduction*, 126, the author remarks that a second-floor room for receiving strangers was called a *murabba‘* in Aleppo, a *tabaqa* in Sidon, and a *qasr* in Damascus. *Tabaqa* is the second floor of a house in Damascus, while most Aleppo houses did not have a second floor at all.

50. *Sijill* 123 (film 222)/pp. 266–67/2 Jumada II 1200: The house had "an inner and an outer [sections]" (*juwwani wa barrani*), the latter having a private entrance, a courtyard with a pool watered by the Qanawat River, an *iwan* (a reception area opening onto the courtyard), a *murabba‘*, a kitchen, a latrine (*murtafaq*), a stone stairwell to a second story (*tabaqa*) with two *qasr*s, and a *mushrifa* (balcony?). The *juwwani* comprised a private entrance, a tiled courtyard with a pool, an *iwan* on the south side, a *qa‘a* (an enclosed reception area) with three *tarzat* (embroideries?), a floor *ardiyya* with a *fisqiyya* (fountain), and a window, an *oda*, a kitchen, a stone stairwell that ascended to three *qasr*s, a kitchen, and a latrine.

51. This issue is often compounded by property segments that involve multiple fractions such as 5 1/2 1/8 1/16 *qirat*s of a property, or even more bewildering, 1/2, 1/4, 1/5 and 1/20 of 18 *qirat*s of a house [*sijill* 123 (film 222)/pp. 429–30/19 dhu'l-Qa‘da 1200]. See also *sijill* 174 (film 209)/Rabi‘ I 1180, in which 9 1/2 1/10 of the north *muqassam,* which represented 1/3 of a house, was sold. Why did the scribes not add these fractions? Is it possible that the fractions referred to different parts of the property? On further thought, is this an early form of time-share ownership?

52. Abdel Nour, *Introduction*, 100; 130–35; Raymond, *Great Arab Cities*, 81–87. See also Marcus, *Middle East*, 282; 317–18.

53. Raymond and others have repeatedly reminded us that the extant Arab houses were not typical—that the vast majority of the humble dwellings have vanished. Given the extent of the segmentation of property, is it conceivable that the typical humble dwelling was in fact the *muqassam* and only rarely the individual one-room structure which has not survived?

54. Jews were involved—mostly as buyers from other Jews—in 15 of the 28 *hawsh* residential purchases. The following is representative: the property sold was

"the northern *murabbaʿ* in Ḥawsh al-Furn in Maḥallat al-Yahud which comprised a door, a window, four walls, a ceiling, the right to use the courtyard, well, and latrine" [*sijill* 218 (film 193)/Muharram 1204]. Among those documents, however, one stands out: the purchase by the head of the Armenian community (*raʾis taʾifat al-arman*) of a whole Muslim-owned *ḥawsh* in Bab Sharqi for 9,000 *qurush*. We may speculate that this particular *ḥawsh* was to be converted into a charitable *waqf* [*sijill* 490/Rabiʿ I 1274].

55. This is most dramatically illustrated in the ratio between entire properties and shares thereof traded between Christians and Jews—the only instance in which the number of whole sales was higher than that of shares: 10 out of the total of 19 transactions between Christians and Jews involved entire properties.

56. The remaining 17 properties had been "bought earlier."

57. Marcus, "Privacy in Eighteenth-Century Aleppo." In a rare document dated May 1782, Shoʿa w. Musa al-Tabbakh and his half-brother Shamuil w. Yaʿqub al-Hilu submitted in court that of the property they had jointly purchased 17 days earlier, they share the property equally, their shares are clearly demarcated, and that henceforth "fully content and open-minded, they have no business with each other's property" [*sijill* 217 (film 193)/21 Jumada II 1196].

58. Conflict over real estate was common, and the lawsuits it brought about are regularly documented in the *sijill*s. Most of these lawsuits were intrafamilial and dealt with the legal fixing of inherited shares and the eviction of relatives and others. In contrast, the *sijill*s are remarkably reticent about the kinds of conflicts that must have arisen among co-inhabitants. For, in addition to the petty feuds that crowding must have engendered, the intercommunal sharing of residences must have raised serious issues involving sumptuary and sexual taboos. If Abdel Nour is correct about the absence of kitchens in most dwellings and the use of the courtyard for cooking, did the sharing of space extend to the sharing of food, for example? Granted that the Christians who co-habitated with Muslims were too poor to afford meat, was pork ever consumed on these premises?

59. Abdel Nour, *Introduction*, 123.

60. The literature on social space is extensive. See, for example, Henri Lefebvre, *The Production of Space*, trans. Donald Nicholson-Smith (Oxford: Blackwell, 1991).

61. On the Arab house see, for example, Raymond, *Great Arab Cities*; George Marcais, "Dar" in *Encyclopedia of Islam*, 2nd ed.; Daniel Panzac, ed., *Les villes dans l'empire Ottoman: Activités et sociétés*, vol. 2 (CNRS, 1994); Dominique Chevallier, "Les villes arabes depuis le XIXe siècle: structure, visions, transformation," in *Villes et travail en Syrie du XIXe au XXe siècle* (Paris: G.-P. Maisonneuve & Larose, 1982); Abdel Nour, "Types architecturaux," in Chevallier, ed., *L'Espace social*; Roberto Berardi, "Espace et ville en pays d'Islam,"

in *L'Espace social*. On the Arab city see A. H. Hourani and S.M. Stern, *The Islamic City: A Colloquium* (Oxford: Bruno Cassirer, 1970). S.M. Stern, "The Constitution of the Islamic City," in *The Islamic City*, ed. Hourani and Stern. Dale E. Eickelman, "Is There an Islamic City? The Making of a Quarter in a Moroccan Town," in *International Journal of Middle Eastern Studies* 5 (1974), 274–94; Ira Marvin Lapidus, *Muslim Cities in the Later Middle Ages* (Cambridge: Harvard University Press, 1967); Baber Johansen, "The All-embracing Town and Its Mosques: al-misr al-gamiꜥ," in *Revue de l'Occident Musulman et de la Méditerranée* 32 (1981–82): 139–55; Kenneth Brown, "The Uses of a Concept: 'The Muslim City'," in *Middle Eastern Cities in Comparative Perspective*, ed. Kenneth Brown, Michèle Jolé, Peter Sluglett, and Sami Zubaida (London: Ithaca Press, 1986).

The Legal Recourse of Minorities in History: Eighteenth-Century Appeals to the Islamic Court of Galata

FATMA MÜGE GÖÇEK

The current problems of minority representation in the former Yugoslavia and the former Soviet Union, South Africa, India, England, and the United States raise significant issues concerning the legal jurisdiction of minorities: how should the rights of these minorities be secured? The nationalist discourse which defines these minorities as equal participants in its imagined community of citizens often fails to guarantee this equality. Yet many instances in history predating nationalism have at least provided, if not equality, some legal recourse to minorities. The legal status of the Greek, Armenian, and Jewish communities of the Ottoman empire is a case in point. In addition to maintaining legal autonomy in communal affairs, the members of these communities also brought some cases to the Islamic court, thereby utilizing both the Islamic and their communal legal system. Little is known about how and when such minority recourse to the Islamic court occurred, however.

This paper focuses on a random sample of three volumes of Galata court registers representing the years 1729, 1769, and 1789 to determine the social pattern behind Ottoman minority recourse to Islamic courts. The selection of the district of Galata in Istanbul, the capital of the empire, controls for the possible factor of geographical proximity as a determinant of choice of court by minorities, as it is almost equidistant from both the Muslim court and the communal courts of the non-Muslims. My analysis reveals that the legal recourse of minorities to the Islamic court of Galata increased throughout the eighteenth century, and that the Ottoman Armenians and Greeks in the Galata district utilized the Islamic court much more than the Ottoman Jews. I argue that it was the intersection of the individual needs of the community members with the boundaries set by the physical space of Galata, the legal space of the Islamic court, and the communal space of legal resolution that determined this diverse intercommunal pattern of non-Muslim recourse to Islamic courts in eighteenth-century Galata.

Historical Sources on Ottoman Minorities

Our knowledge of the internal dynamics of the non-Muslim communities in the Ottoman empire is still fragmentary. The Armenians, Greeks, and Jews who formed the three main non-Muslim minorities[1] in the Ottoman empire had protected legal status as ethnic-religious communities. Each was granted some internal autonomy, and had to pay a special protection and military exemption tax in return. This internal autonomy often comprised the right to elect communal administrators to oversee communal property, to adjudicate conflict within the community, and to represent the community to the Ottoman state at large. The legal adjudication of disputes was often perceived as the most significant right and responsibility of the community.

Imperial decrees and religious opinions concerning minorities have often been taken as indicators of communal behavior in the Ottoman empire. The scholarship and the sources it utilizes produce the following portrait. Imperial decrees throughout the eighteenth century (Ahmet Refik 1930: 30–31, 88–89, 83–84) command, for instance, that "Christians should not reside in the vicinity of the mosque in Galata," "Jews should not inhabit buildings near the Yeni Cami mosque," or "Christians and Jews should have shorter buildings than

Muslims." The religious opinions of distinguished Muslim scholars of their times, such as those of Ebussuud Efendi in the sixteenth century (Düzdağ 1983: 94, 99), contain opinions on such questions as "Is it permissible to rent to a Jew a house which has inscribed on its wall verses from the Qur'an?" or "If Zeyd the Jew goes from Istanbul proper to Galata to conduct business and if Amr the Christian, claiming [Zeyd the Jew] needs to settle a transaction, takes him to the Islamic court of Galata, would Zeyd the Jew have the right to state that he wants the case heard instead by the Islamic court in his neighborhood in Istanbul proper?" The response is negative in the first case and affirmative in the second. Similarly, specific studies on the position of non-Muslim minorities in the Ottoman empire mostly focus on imperial decrees and law codes in the fifteenth and sixteenth centuries (Ercan 1983), land surveys and population registers in the eighteenth century (Özkaya 1985), poll-tax registers of non-Muslims in the eighteenth and nineteenth centuries (Bağış 1983), statistical surveys (Eryılmaz 1990) and constitutional law (Bozkurt 1989) during the late nineteenth and early twentieth centuries. Some others concentrate on the interaction of non-Muslim minorities with foreign merchants (Mantran 1982, Davison 1982), or with Muslims (Findley 1982).

These studies on non-Muslim communities in the Ottoman empire often point to legal restrictions rather than actual behavior, however. It is in this context that the Islamic court records of individual cases brought to court reveal the delicate link between theory and legal practice. Works on Ottoman court records of such scholars as Halil İnalcık (1953–54), L. Fekete (1965), Abdulkarim Rafeq (1966), Jon Mandeville (1966), Amnon Cohen (1973, 1984), Ronald Jennings (1975, 1978), Yuzo Nagata (1976a, 1976b), Yavuz Cezar (1977), Bernard Lewis (1984), Giles Veinstein (1979, 1981), Haim Gerber (1980), Abraham Marcus (1983), Murat Çizakça (1985), Beshara Doumani (1985), Judith Tucker (1986), Tülay Artan (1989), and Yvonne Seng (1991) are therefore crucial in demonstrating Ottoman legal practice in everyday life, and the frequent minority utilization of the Islamic court.[2] Islamic court records thus reflect the entire Ottoman experience by covering all segments of Ottoman society. A systematic analysis of this archival source through random sampling would help explore the nature and scope of court use by different segments of the populace.

Methodological Issues in the Employment of Court Records

The most significant contribution of court records to historical analysis is the information they provide on the lives of ordinary people.[3] The significance of court records for sociological analysis centers on the social spectrum they cover. By providing information on the underclasses, these records disclose the entire social structure and facilitate the analysis of all social groups in a society. Yet, a word of caution is necessary here: court records in and of themselves do not have any explanatory power unless they are randomly sampled and interpreted within a theoretical context. Also, these records only permit inferences and only approximate possible patterns of social behavior.

The Ottoman court records can be used as the unit of historical socio-logical analysis only after their historical contextualization, that is, after their social, spatial and temporal placement within Ottoman society. The origins of these court records can be traced to Islamic law which mainly consists of the maxims laid down in the Qur'an,[4] the prescriptions of the Prophet in his teachings, and the pre-Islamic customs prevailing among the Arab tribes near Mecca and Medina (Chowdury 1964; Coulson 1971). The Ottomans accepted the Ḥanafī school of interpretation of the Qur'anic prescriptions and used Ibrāhīm al-Ḥalebī's *Multaqā al-abḥur* as the source-book in apply-ing Islamic law. Ottoman practice closely followed the general principles laid down by the law, with some practical qualifications. A judge (*kadı*)[5] at the religious court heard the cases and adjudicated.[6] The legal organization reflected the Ottoman stratification between officials and subjects as separate judges oversaw the sultan's officials and his subjects. Ottoman officials had their own "military" (*askerî*) judges, as opposed to subjects, who had "local" (*beledî*) judges. The military judges did not reside in each judicial district like the local ones, but resided in Constantinople instead and listened to cases at the sultan's palace on Tuesdays and Wednesdays and at their residences the rest of the week. The cases these judges adjudicated over the centuries throughout the empire form a vast source of information on social life.

Since Ottoman court records exist in vast numbers, I employed a sam-pling method to draw cases that would both address my research question and also be representative of Ottoman society at large. The employment of the sampling method does have certain limitations, however. First, the sample population: the court records were drawn up only upon the request of the parties and therefore did not include either those cases settled without judiciary assistance or those cases which belonged to anyone who could not afford to bring cases to court. The sample population is therefore biased toward large and complicated cases and does not cover the target population of all the inheritance cases in eighteenth-century Ottoman society. Second, the nature of the court records: they are often incomplete. All the information about a case is sometimes spread out under separate entries within one or more registers. Hence the sampling of cases may fail to capture the judicial process in its entirety. In spite of these problems, however, the court records are a significant historical source in Ottoman social history since they contain detailed individual-level information about Ottoman society that expands beyond the material in the official state correspondence for and by the administrators, and in travelers' accounts for and by Westerners.

Islamic Court Records of Eighteenth-Century Galata

The sampling method I employed comprised a number of stages. Given my query into the minority access to Islamic courts, I needed to focus on major cities that had both Islamic and minority courts. The capital of the empire, Constantinople, provided one such significant context where the communal courts coexisted with Islamic ones and minorities thus had access to both. Within the context of Constantinople, I needed to focus on local rather than military court records since the minorities were not permitted to join this social group in the empire. Since geographical constraints could influence the use of one court over the other, I had to select within Constantinople a district that contained both communal and Islamic courts within traveling distance. According to the archives of the Istanbul court records located at the Office of the Religious Opinion (*Müftülük*), in the course of the eighteenth century, the city of Constantinople had the follwing Islamic courts: Kasımpaşa, Üsküdar, Ahi Çelebi, Davut Paşa, Bakırköy, Kartal, Adalar, Beykoz, Galata, Havass-ı Refia (Eyüp), Balat, Yeniköy, Hasköy, Beşiktaş, Tophane, and Mahmut Paşa.

Among these, in the eighteenth century, Galata contained both Islamic and communal courts as well as Muslim and minority populations. After its establishment in the late fifteenth century, the Islamic court of Galata was one of the most important courts in the Istanbul area, especially for the inhabitants on the western side of the city (Yazgan 1988). Not only was Galata's court the main seat of justice for the province of Rum's coast, but the court deputies of three hundred villages and forty administrative districts including Kasımpaşa and Beşiktaş were subject to the judge of Galata as well (Uzunçarşılı 1984: 133–34).

In order to draw my sample, I selected the period from 1705 to 1809, the century before Mahmud II and the major reforms of the Tanzimat era that radically altered the judicial system. I randomly selected, from three clusters of approximately thirty-five years, the registers corresponding to the years 1729, 1769, and 1789, and studied these in their entirety.[7] The register from 1729 contained 275 cases, most of which were inheritance cases with a few property disputes; the 1769 register contained 182 cases; and the register from 1789 included 246 cases. In these records, non-Muslim oarsmen as well as moneychangers, porters as well as furriers, fishermen and chief translators appeared on the same page as Muslim itinerant coffee sellers, subjects in the service of the head of the palace doorkeepers, and janissaries. The range of litigants can be illustrated with several examples from my sample. For instance, the *dalyancı*, a fisherman attached to a fishing station raised on poles above the water, known as Mihail son of Zahir (14/493, #8) had the distinction of being the poorest Christian found in these documents. He owned only two pairs of baggy trousers and a sheep-lined cloak, in addition to 732 *akçe*s. In sharp contrast, the Armenian translator Musan son of Hursadr (14/395, #162) owned eight fur coats, a horse, and 1,711,852 *akçe*s. The wife of the Armenian tailor Mgırdıç son of Karabet, Tamank daughter of Boghos (14/493, #24), had an estate valued at 3,555 *akçe* of mostly clothing, bedding, and a trunk upon her death, whereas the Armenian Serpuhi, daughter of Mardaros, (14/493, #133) had an estate worth 154,520 *akçe*s of which one-third was diamond jewelry and 12,000 *akçe* was in cash.

Raw data on the social and economic conditions of non-Muslim subjects found in Islamic court records thus contain information on material goods, source and location of wealth, property ownership, quarter of residence, religion, gender, children, family, gender of the steward of the estate and guardian of minors, and value of goods. These records establish social and economic patterns in Ottoman society that are more representative of all classes and religio-ethnic affiliation than other official Ottoman sources. In addition to the socioeconomic data, patterns of non-Muslim decision-making can also be gleaned from the records.

Social Boundaries of Minority Participation in Ottoman Society

In Ottoman society, subjects were identified as Armenian, Orthodox, Jewish, and Muslim semi-autonomous ethno-religious communities administered by a recognized religious authority and communal council. It is important to note that the Orthodox community was predominantly Greek in Istanbul, but Arab in the Arabophone provinces and Serbian in the Balkans. The Muslim community included Turks, Kurds, Arabs, and many other distinct communities. The Jewish community had no recognized leader who had any authority outside of Istanbul, whereas the Armenian and Orthodox church hierarchies allowed a patriarch; the Muslims were represented by the Seyhülislâm. The courts were situated within the communal space in which they functioned. In return for paying a poll-tax, *cizye*, members of non-Muslim communities were excused from military service and hence placed themselves under the protection of the Sultan. In return for paying the *cizye*, the adherents of recognized religious communities were allowed to work and worship freely, and to live according to the rules of their own religion as long as they symbolically declared that Islam was the superior religion through various, yet often un-enforced, sumptuary laws. The autonomous religio-ethnic status was especially noticeable within Ottoman urban centers as the different communities tended to group together in particular neighborhoods, although the neighborhoods were not exclusive to one community.

Within this legal and communal framework, my research shows that radically increasing numbers of inheritances of Armenian and Greek subjects appear in the court records over the century while those of Jews, who should have had many reasons to seek legal recourse at the Islamic court, do not appear. Confirming previous studies, my analysis indicates that non-Muslims frequently used the Islamic court. Non-Muslims represented 2.9% of all cases in 1729, but 28.3% by 1788. I conjecture that non-Muslims who were both dissatisfied with the inheritance partitioning within the context of their local communities, and willing to defy the hold of the communal courts and taxing authority, brought cases to the Islamic court.

(i) Minorities within the Physical Space of Galata.

The specific historical and demographical background of Galata in Istanbul constructed the physical space and influenced the course of action of Ottoman non-Muslims. Galata is a particularly significant city to study since the existence of large non-Muslim communities and the proximity to non-Muslim and Muslim courts allows me to study their decisions concerning adjudication. Galata, separated from the predominantly Muslim and Turkish part of Constantinople by the Golden Horn and from the Asian part by the Bosphorus, had been a Genoese commercial colony under Byzantine rule (Arseven 1989, Mantran 1982). Following Sultan Mehmet's conquest in 1453, Galata retained its Christian character as it transformed itself from an Italian and Greek city to a cosmopolitan trading center with Greek, Armenian, and Jewish merchants, foreign traders, middlemen, and European embassies.

With the Armenians and remaining Latins, Galata had a Christian majority and a Muslim minority. Indeed, non-Muslim identity in Constantinople in general and in Galata in particular persisted. In 1830, for instance, Constantinople had fifty-four Greek churches, forty-three Armenian churches and neighborhoods, and eighteen Jewish neighborhoods (Karpat 1985: 202). The existence of an Armenian quarter in Galata centered around St. Gregory the Illuminator church, established in 1391 and recorded in the Ottoman survey of 1455, attests to the continuation of the Byzantine Armenian presence into the Ottoman period (İnalcık 1991: 35).

A survey conducted in 1478 shows that the Greeks were the largest community in Galata with 592 households, followed by 535 Muslim and 62 Armenian households (İnalcık 1991: 97). Notebooks of the businesses and homes and the religio-ethnic identity of their owners, mapped for the Sultan's boat trips around the coast of Galata in the mid-to-late fifteenth century (*bostancı başı defterleri*), corroborate the existence of a dense Armenian concentration in the eastern half of Galata (Üyepazarcı 1992: 110–14). Indeed, some scholars have argued that Galata "had been the living heart of the Armenian community" (Kevorkian and Pabudjian 1992: 99). In the eighteenth century, the residences of Ottoman Armenians spread in all directions except for western Galata, and moved well beyond the Byzantine core north, west, and eastward into Kasımpaşa, Dört Yol/Pera, Beşiktaş and Tophane. From church buildings and the Sultan's boat trip maps, I know that Greeks were also concentrated in eastern and central Galata in the late fifteenth century. Decrees prohibiting the construction of housing by non-Muslims in eighteenth-century Beşiktaş, Ortaköy, and Tophane point to a sizeable and growing Christian presence although the Greeks remained the "largest non-Muslim population on the European shore of the Bosphorus" (Artan 1989: 163, 189). An early-nineteenth-century English map denotes a "Jewish ward" in eastern Galata as well, and the sultan's boat trip notebooks also confirm a significant number of Jewish households in the area. Furthermore, the quarters of residence recorded in the inheritance records show that Armenians and Greeks lived in Tophane, Beşiktaş, Dört Yol/Pera, Kasımpaşa, and quarters in eastern Galata itself, especially Sultan Bayezid and Bereketzade. The only concrete data I have on numbers of Armenians, Greeks, Jews, and Muslims are drawn from the 1927 census, which points to the Greeks as the largest community in Galata (İnalcık 1991: 105, Üyepazarcı 1992: 110–14, Atlas 1836).

Eighteenth-century Galata court records confirm the spatial concentration of non-Muslims in the eastern half of Galata. The western half contained the court in a neighborhood anchored by the Arab Mosque. In 1711, a French traveler described the area as a Muslim quarter (Ortaylı 1989: 133). One would not want to leave the reader with the impression that the quarters were rigidly Armenian, Greek, Jewish, or Muslim, however. The court records demonstrate that Armenians and Greeks lived in the same quarter as Muslims, for example, in Bereketzade in eastern Galata. Nevertheless, it can be stated that eastern Galata was predominantly Christian, as was Galata as a whole. The court's location in a predominantly Muslim neighborhood did not hinder non-Muslims in bringing their appeal to the Islamic court for justice.

Court records indicate that, in the eighteenth century, Galata retained its distinction as a cosmopolitan trading center with Greek, Armenian, and Jewish merchants. The occupations of the subjects listed in my sample of non-Muslim inheritance registers point to many artisans who chose to reside in Galata and engaged in trade. Of the non-Muslims in my sample who came to this court in the middle and end of the century, 38% and 48% of men were artisans, and 58% and 39% were merchants, in 1769 and 1789 respectively. For instance, the Armenian grocer Avak son of Boghos (14/395, #118) owned his own store, which was one-sixth of his estate. All but a few of the Armenians and Greeks were merchants of timber, flour, soap, tobacco, and oil, and artisans such as tailors, furriers, and carpenters. The full list of artisans includes barbers, stone-masons, printers of cloth, stone-cutters, metal cutters, clothiers, gardeners, makers of fish nets and augers. The full list of merchants includes fruit-drink sellers, grocers and greengrocers, butchers, store owners, sesame-oil sellers, vegetable vendors, wine sellers, millers, and shoeshines.

(ii) Minorities within the Legal Space of the Islamic Court.

When a non-Muslim entered a Muslim court in Istanbul two hundred years ago, subtle language within the texts recorded by the scribe identified Christians and Jews in distinction to Muslims. The language deployed in the text reflects and reproduces the status of non-Muslims in the social hierarchy of eighteenth century Galata. The systematic deployment of certain language was crucial in determining and reproducing the symbolic boundaries of identity within the Ottoman empire. At the same that judges upheld the rights of non-Muslims who appealed to them for justice, they did so by deploying language and categories which reconfirmed non-Muslims' status within the social structure. Although non-Muslims appeared in court, had property rights, and often owned substantial estates, the court language privileged the societal status of male Muslims over non-Muslim males, and female Muslims over non-Muslim females.

In my sample, only 3 out of the 128 documents involving Christians refer to the claimants or to the deceased as "Christian." Only 2 of the 55 Armenians are referred to as "Armenian," and only 3 of the 73 Greeks were called "Greek." However, the lone Jewish claimant in my sample, Katyana daughter of Judah (14/493, #71) from Beşiktaş, is referred to as a Jew as is her father. The scribe clearly states Stephan son of Yorgi's identity (14/268, #14) as "the one who perished in unbelief being Stephan son of Yorgi son of Asarmank, a Christian name." In another case (14/268, #49), Zoi daughter of Persek is described as "the one with the Christian name," whereas the man who inherits from her, Petro son of Manos, is called a "dhimmi." These are rare cases, however. The prevailing pattern in these documents is not to use the terms "Christian," "Armenian," or "Greek."

However, certain language is deployed by the scribe that, even without such a label as "Christian," delineates the fact that the individual in question was not a Muslim. In the texts, a Muslim man was most often given honorifics such as *hacı, efendi, çelebi, emin, paşa.* Non-Muslim men were referred to by occupational status. Muslim women were referred to as *hatun,* lady. Non-Muslim women were defined through their husband's occupational standing. The texts did not use such terms for pejorative reasons, but repeated the social segmentation of society. More specifically, the first several lines forming a Muslim woman's inheritance refers to the woman as "one who had been living or dwelling in a certain neighborhood *(sakine)*," followed by the name of the woman prefaced by the honorific title "lady *(hatun)*," whom "God drew back to Himself *(vefat eden)*." In contrast, the first two lines of a non-Muslim woman's inheritance read as "one who had settled in a place *(mütemekkin)*," succeeded by the name of the woman without any honorific titles, who "perished in unbelief *(halike olan)*." Although not referred to as "infidel" *(kâfir)*, nevertheless there certainly is a great difference in being gathered back to God upon death and in expiring like fruit. Furthermore, to live or dwell in a place sounds more dignified than settling in like a late guest. A male Muslim is the "son of a certain man *(ibn ül)*," whereas a non-Muslim male is the "child of a certain man *(veled-i)*."

The legal language of the inheritance of the Armenian razor-maker, Sahak son of Abraham, demonstrates this portrayal of minorities (14/493, #43). The court record reads in part:

> In the city of Galata domiciled in Sultan Bayezid neighborhood, the razor-maker Sahak son of Abraham perished in unbelief with debts which were greater than his estate . . . in accordance with Islamic law, his inheritance is limited to his wives, Lalab daughter of [illegible] and Huri daughter of Artin, and his sister from the same father, Hanım, and his sister from the same mother, Suhuman. The aforementioned Lalab and Huri and Hanım and Suhuman are mentioned as creditors in the claiming and requesting the registration of and paying the debt of the estate of the aforementioned perished one.

I note that in this particular text, a man, defined by profession, father's name, and his lack of true faith, has his estate registered by his surviving relatives, who submit the inheritance to a Muslim judge to dispense with according to Islamic law. Like many entries of unbelievers, the correct spelling, vocalization, and rendering of those with Armenian, Greek, or Hebrew names in the text is often an unsatisfactory endeavor since their names were often altered beyond recognition—if not spelled different ways in the same document—as the names were transformed into Ottoman script. For instance, the name of the Armenian translator's wife (14/395, #162) is spelled three different ways in the text. The systematic deployment of formulaic terms which distinguish non-Muslims from Muslims thus reflect and reproduce the societal difference between the Muslims and the rest.

(iii) Minorities within the Communal Space of Legal Resolution.

Our sample reveals that during the eighteenth century, radically increasing numbers of Ottoman Armenians and Greeks bypassed their communal courts and took their inheritances instead to the Islamic court. Whereas Christians comprised two percent of all cases heard there in the beginning of the century in my 1729 sample, the proportion of Christians taking their cases to the Islamic court of Galata had increased to thirty percent of all cases heard in 1789. Only a few cases involved any other issue than inheritance, and these were exclusively property disputes and sales. The Armenians and Greeks appear often in these court records, at times more Armenians than Greeks in a given year and vice-versa, but always in rising numbers over the century: seven Greeks in 1729 and forty-six in 1769, for example.

The number of Armenians and Greeks who came to court to register the inheritances was at least three times the number of the deceased. The size of Galata's Armenian and Greek population increased over the century significantly. Although the precise extent of the growth cannot be determined, the increase cannot have been as proportionately large as the proportionate increase in court usage. Even though cases involving the inheritances of men were always frequent, there was a marked increase in the number and proportion of cases involving deceased non-Muslim women also increased, from one-third to over one-half. It is clear that Christian men and women went to the court to press their inheritance claims. The numerical breakdown of the documents is as follows: of the 703 cases, 18% concerned non-Muslims; 72% of the non-Muslim cases concerned males. The number of cases concerning non-Muslims rose precipitously during the century, nearly sixfold from 1729 to 1769 and another 50% to 1789; 6% of those appearing were non-Muslims in 1729, 39% in 1769 and 55% in 1789.

These figures need to be understood within the context of the Ottoman legal system, which allowed Muslim, Armenian, Orthodox, and Jewish courts to flourish. The rulers of the empire employed a multi-tiered court system for their subjects. In addition to the Muslim courts, which ruled by Ḥanafī law and custom on personal matters including inheritance, marriage, divorce, custody, and guardianship for all members of society, the Jews and the recognized Christian communities at the time—Armenians and the Greek Orthodox—had their own courts, which were free to administer justice in all matters except criminal cases. The Christian and Jewish leadership could excommunicate, banish, fine, and chastise their members concerning internal matters, but not in issues involving Muslims and Muslim authority.

The non-Muslim courts adjudicated disputes within the communities; most cases involved inheritances and disputes over the sale of property and personal matters such as marriage. For instance, for the Armenian community, "the patriarch was allowed his own court and prison at the capital for trying members of the community in all cases except those involving 'public security and crime' [and he] had jurisdiction in matters of personal status, divorce, inheritance, guardianship, and no Ottoman official could interfere in his decisions" (Artinian 1988: 15–16). The Greek jurisdiction was similar. Their patriarch was also "invested with rights of a purely civil character (to exercise judicial powers) against laymen among whom divergences may arise in connection with everything that related to marriage, divorce, and the like" (Papadopoullos 1990: 33–34). The Jewish community also had its law court (*bet din*). The head of the Jews, according to one historical document (Goitein 1970: 115), decided, "as the highest legal authority, all matters of marriage and divorce, supervised the moral and religious conduct of his flock, including the general authority of ordering people to act properly and to prevent them from acting improperly, imposed and removed bans and orders of excommunication, expounded authoritatively on the Scriptures, either orally or in responsa, appointed and dismissed judges, cantors and other religious officials and defined their rights and duties, supervised the actions of social service officers and other persons holding public office, and sometimes delegated his authority in any town or country to any reliable person chosen by him."

Within the Ottoman legal system, multiple spaces of adjudication for different minority communities thus existed alongside each other. One would expect these non-Muslims to adhere to the decisions of their leaders and to have little reason not to do so. Legal adjudication was perceived by the Christian and Jewish community leaders, if not by the lay persons, as one of their most significant rights and responsibilities and as a location in which to exercise their power. Decisions pertaining to non-Muslim property and personal matters were made by their leaders, as individual members of the community related to the central government through their community, which was responsible for intracommunal legal matters. Yet, in spite of this communal legal system, why did many minorities seek adjudication in the Islamic courts? Also, why were there differences among the Ottoman Greeks, Armenians, and Jews in court usage? If these communities had viewed Muslim judicial authorities with the force of the Sultan and army and governing authority behind them as a final arbiter bearing much more weight in their decisions than their communal courts, why would not all communities have utilized Islamic courts to the same degree?

Non-Muslim cases might have been brought to court because of the relatively unfair shares given to non-Muslims according to their communal laws of inheritance vis-à-vis the Muslim shares. According to the Islamic law of inheritance, women were guaranteed shares not allowed, for example, in Jewish law. Jewish women could not divorce their husbands according to Jewish law; Jewish daughters received considerably less than Muslim daughters in inheritances. I would expect Jewish men and women, not an insignificant population in eighteenth-century Galata, to appear in the Islamic court to register and to seek shares of inheritances not allowed by Jewish law. Only one Jewish inheritance was recorded in my sample, however. Another study on Jews in Istanbul during this period notes that the Jews used the Islamic courts in settling commercial disputes, not in cases concerning personal law; it lists only one inheritance case in which the sons of the deceased declared before the Muslim judge that they had all received their fair share in the inheritance and that there were no other claimants (Gerber 1982: 31). According to the same study, Christians most often came to the court for the purposes of marriage and conversion to Islam.

Perhaps Galata Jews took their cases to courts elsewhere, or, more likely, the silence in my sample displays the effective social control of the Jewish communal leaders over their members,[8] one not displayed to the same degree by the Armenian and Greek communal leadership. Until 1908, the main Jewish court was located in a synagogue in Balat, across the Golden Horn from Galata. The chief rabbi in Istanbul during my earliest sample of 1729 was Samuel Levi, a rabbi of notable distinction, whose communal presence may have prevented the Jewish subjects in the area from bringing their cases to the Islamic court (Galante 1985: 247). Furthermore, the chief rabbi was sometimes the judge at the *bet din*, i.e. the leader of the law court, whose authority was so great that "it could even enforce (itself) on those who wished to withdraw from the court" and its authority (Galante 1985: 221). One could argue that the rabbinical hold over the Ottoman Jewish community, which increased after the Sabbatai Sevi incident, lasted until the end of the Ottoman empire.[9] Indeed, among the three minority communities, the Jewish traditional leadership as exercised by the rabbis of the community (Epstein 1982: 101) far outlasted that of the Greeks and Armenians, which were quickly overtaken by lay leadership.

Yet the tension between the leadership and the community was also ever-present (Dumont 1982). Additional evidence of the tension between the power of religious authorities to induce and maintain order in their community and that of the individual to avoid it comes from the Jewish community of Izmir. Haim Falaji, a mid-nineteenth-century rabbi, lamented that "there is no power in the hands of the rabbis" as the Jews avoided the decisions of the *bet din* (Barnai 1982: 59). He further mourned the "chaos" that ensued as individuals "did what their hearts desire" and ended up evading paying their share of the community's tax obligation to the Ottoman authorities (Barnai 1982: 60). The communal order was rent as the rabbis could not impose their will. Still, they were able to force all members of the community to sign an agreement not to go outside the authority of the *bet din* or risk excommunication, though such a document was rarely put into practice (Barnai 1982: 58). Yet, I should also note that the high degree of effective communication and coordination between Jewish and Muslim courts (Goitein 1970: 116) may be another factor explaining the infrequent Jewish use of the Islamic court in Galata.

The condition of the leadership of the Armenian and Greek communities was much different during this period. The Greek community at the time was experiencing a crisis in authority (Frangakis 1985). After 1763 I see an explosion in the number of Greeks coming to the court in Galata, which is certainly related to "the loss of the effective authority of the Patriarch, and the reduction of the authority of the officials to insignificance" (Papado-poullos 1990: 59). Indeed, lay representatives assumed authority and aided the reorganization of the community in the nineteenth century (Augustinos 1992: 125). The decrease in the authority of the patriarch is noted especially as some members stopped paying their share of the communal taxes; the metropolitan of Nicea wrote, on one occasion, to the patriarch in Istanbul that "it would be desirable if his Holiness took steps to . . . send an order to them because their behavior is scandalous for the others" (Augustinos 1992: 137). This increasing rupture between the religious and lay leadership would certainly have allowed and encouraged the Ottoman Greeks to seek justice in the Islamic court.

Less is known about the Armenian patriarchate, although one can conjecture that a similar crisis also occurred within this non-Muslim community as the increasing tension between the clergy and laypeople in assuming communal leadership peaked during the course of the eighteenth century. Armenian literati did indeed "battle against the entrenched forces (of the Armenian religious authorities) in an effort to democratize their institutions" (Sarkiss 1937: 447). The lay intervention in patriarchate affairs started in 1612 when a group of laymen, led by the influential Hoca Astuocatur, "reacted against the despotic rule of Grigor Kesaraci and demanded his resignation and replaced him with Zakaria Veneci" (Artinian 1989: 27). The significance of the Armenian laity increased especially after 1725 when "the Patriarch Hovhannes Kolot called a general assembly to elect a new catholicos for all Armenians and invited, in addition to the high ranking clergy and magnates, the leaders of all the Armenian guilds[10] in Constantinople" (Artinian 1981: 193; 1989: 28). By the end of the eighteenth century, there were 65 Armenian guilds, and these had doubled in size by the second quarter of the nineteenth century (Artinian 1989: 24). The wealthy leaders of the Armenian community continued to acquire a much stronger presence in the eighteenth and nineteenth centuries as they accumulated large fortunes through their association with the Ottoman government, especially in the fields of finance and industry (Barsoumian 1982: 171; Artinian 1981). These influential Armenians either lent capital to Ottoman officials and individuals on interest to secure appointments and revenue collection, or were directly employed by the Ottoman government as directors of imperial powderworks and textile manufacturing and as architects (Artinian 1989: 21). The religious tension among the Catholic, Orthodox, and Protestant churches within the Armenian community also enhanced the fragmentation (Artinian 1989: 40).

In addition to these communal factors that affected the course of legal action taken by individual minority members, one could also conjecture that during the course of the eighteenth century and later, some individuals in all minority communities no longer saw themselves as members of a subject religio-ethnic community, but rather started to identify themselves either with the Ottoman authority itself or with foreign embassies. A case in point are the minority merchants who started to trade under the protection of Western powers (Bağış 1983). In my sample, the three wealthy translators, Musan son of Hursadr (14/395, #162), the translator to the French embassy Dominick Kurtani son of Conyateste and Dominick's son Karlo (14/268, #14), could be such examples of minorities who ended up bestowing their allegiance on their European employers rather than on their communities or Ottoman society at large. Many individuals could also be seen as the emerging members of a new bourgeoisie whose new forms of wealth outside of the communal leadership's control bestowed upon them in the nineteenth century a new consciousness that trespassed communal boundaries (Göçek, 1996). For instance, the Greek ship captain (*re'is*) Dimitri son of Dimo could be an example of this phenomenon (14/493, #29).

Conclusion

The individual minorities who came to the Islamic court thus seem to have enacted their needs within the boundaries set by their interpretation of their physical, legal, and communal space. The significance of individual needs in setting the boundaries of legal action is demonstrated by Dale Eickelman when he argues that social structure ought to be "conceived with individuals as the fundamental units of social structure rather than their attributes or statuses as members of groups" (Eickelman 1974: 281). Members of the minority communities of Galata do indeed illustrate the deployment of "tactics" of manipulation of identity and institutions to gain the best advantage for oneself (de Certau 1984) as individual Armenians, Greeks, and Jews acted or did not act according to the assumed benefit or loss of using the Islamic court or their own. They were acting outside of their community, taking advantage of their greater subjectness, not to their birth-identity, but to their membership in the total city of Galata. Yet, the physical, legal and communal space did nevertheless determine the social boundaries of their individual needs as they interpreted and took legal action within these constraints.

To return to the issue with which I started, namely the possible minority legal recourse in contemporary situations, I conclude by arguing that only by analyzing the practices of everyday life and the structures of physical, legal, and communal space can one determine how to enhance minority participation in society.

Selected Bibliography

Ahmet Refik (Altınay). 1930. *Hicrî Onikinci Asırda İstanbul Hayatı* (Life in Istanbul during the 18th century), İstanbul: Devlet Matbassı.
Anderson, Benedict. 1983. *Imagined Communities: Reflections on the Origin and Spread of Nationalism*, London: Verso.
Arseven, Celal Esad. 1989. *Eski Galata ve Binaları* (Old Galata and its buildings), İstanbul: Çelik Gülersoy Vakfı, İstanbul Kütüphanesi.
Artan, Tülay. 1989. *Architecture as a Theatre of Life: Profile of the Eighteenth Century Bosphorus*. Ph.D. dissertation, MIT.
Artinian, Vartan. 1988. *The Armenian Constitutional System in the Ottoman Empire, 1839–1863: A Study of Its Historical Development*, İstanbul: [s.n.].
Artinian, Vartan. 1981. "The Role of the Amiras in the Ottoman Empire," *Armenian Review* 34/2-134:189–94.
Atlas of the Society for the Dissemination of Useful Knowledge, 1836. London.
Augustinos, Gerasimos. 1992. *The Greeks of Asia Minor: Confession, Community, and Ethnicity in the Nineteenth Century*, Kent, Ohio: Kent State University Press.
Bağış, Ali İhsan. 1983. *Osmanlı Ticaretinde Gayrî Müslimler* (Non-Muslims in Ottoman trade), Ankara: Turhan Kitapları.
Bardakjian, Kevork. 1982. "The Rise of the Armenian Patriarchate of Constantinople." Vol. 1, pp. 89–100 in B. Braude and B. Lewis, eds. *Christians and Jews in the Ottoman Empire: The Functioning of a Plural Society*. New York: Holmes & Meier.
Barnai, Ya'akov. 1982. "Kavim le-Toledot ha-Hevrah ha-Yehudit be-Izmir be-Shelhei ha-Me'ah ha-18 u-ve-Reshit ha-19" (Notes on the Jewish Community of Izmir at the End of the Eighteenth and Beginning of the Nineteenth Centuries), *Tsiyon* 47:56–76.
Barsoumian, Hagop. 1982. "The Dual Role of the Armenian Amira Class within the Ottoman Government and the Armenian Millet." Vol. 1, pp. 171–84 in B. Braude and B. Lewis, eds. *Christians and Jews in the Ottoman Empire: The Functioning of a Plural Society*. New York: Holmes & Meier.

Bayındır, Abdülaziz. 1984. "Teorik ve Pratik Osmanlı Muhakeme Hukuku" (The Ottoman legal system in theory and practice). Ph.D. dissertation, Erzurum University.

Bourdieu, Pierre. 1984. *Distinction: A Social Critique of the Judgement of Taste.* Translated by Richard Nice. Cambridge, Mass: Harvard University Press.

Bozkurt, Gülnihal. 1989. *Alman-İngiliz Belgelerinin ve Siyasî Gelişmelerin Işığı altında Gayrımüslim Osmanlı Vatandaşlarının Hukuki Durumu (1839–1914)* (The legal position of non-Muslim Ottoman citizens (1839–1914) under the light of German-English documents and political developments), Ankara: Türk Tarih Kurumu.

Braude, Benjamin. 1982. "Foundation Myths of the Millet System." Vol. 1, pp. 69–88 in B. Braude and B. Lewis, eds. *Christians and Jews in the Ottoman Empire: The Functioning of a Plural Society.* New York: Holmes & Meier.

Cahen, Claude. 1960–. "Dhimma." New edition. Vol. 2, pp. 227–231. *Encyclopedia of Islam*, Leiden: E. J. Brill.

de Certeau, Michel. 1984. *The Practice of Everyday Life.* Translated by Steven Randall. Berkeley: University of California Press.

Cezar, Yavuz. 1977. "Bir Ayanın Muhallefatı: Havza ve Köprü Kazaları Ayan? Kör İsmailoğlu Hüseyin" (The inheritance register of an Ottoman provincial notable: Kör İsmailoğlu Hüseyin), *Belleten* 41:41–78.

Chowdury, Sultanul Alam. 1964. "The Problem of Representation in Muslim Law of Inheritance," *Islamic Studies* 3:375–91.

Cohen, Amnon. 1984. *Jewish Life under Islam: Jerusalem in the Sixteenth Century,* Cambridge, Mass.: Harvard University Press.

Cohen, Amnon. 1973. *Palestine in the 18th Century: Patterns of Government and Administration,* Jerusalem: Magnes Press, Hebrew University.

Coulson, Noel J. 1971. *Succession in the Muslim Family,* Cambridge: Cambridge University Press.

Çizakça, Murat. 1985. "Incorporation of the Middle East into the European World Economy," *Review: Journal of the Fernand Braudel Center for the Study of Economics, Historical Systems, and Civilizations* 8:353–78.

Davison, Roderic. 1982. "The Millets as Agents of Change in the 19th Century Ottoman Empire." Vol. 1, pp. 319–37 in B. Braude and B. Lewis, eds. *Christians and Jews in the Ottoman Empire: The Functioning of a Plural Society.* New York: Holmes & Meier.

Doumani, Beshara. 1985. "Palestinian Islamic Court Records: A Source for Socioeconomic History," *Middle Eastern Studies Association Bulletin* 19:155–72.

Düzdağ, M.E. 1983. *Şeyhülislâm Ebussuud Efendi Fetvalar Işığında 16cı Asır Türk Hayatı* (Sixteenth-century Turkish life in the light of the religious opinions of Şeyhülislam Ebussuud Efendi), İstanbul: Enderun Kitabevi.

Eickelman, Dale F. 1974. "Is There an Islamic City? The Making of a Quarter in a Moroccan Town," *International Journal of Middle Eastern Studies* 5:274–94.

Epstein, Mark A. 1982. "The Leadership of the Ottoman Jews in the 15th and 16th Centuries." Vol. 1, pp. 101–15 in B. Braude and B. Lewis, eds. *Christians and Jews in the Ottoman Empire: The Functioning of a Plural Society.* New York: Holmes & Meier.

Ercan, Yavuz. 1983. "Türkiye'de 15 ve 16cı Yüzyıllarda Gayrı Müslimlerin Hukuki, İçtimai ve İktisadi Durumu" (The legal, social, and economic conditions of non-Muslims in fifteenth- and sixteenth century Turkey), *Belleten* 47:1119–49.

Eryılmaz, Bilal. 1990. *Osmanlı Devletinde Gayrımüslim Teb'anın Yönetimi* (The administration of the non-Muslim subjects in the Ottoman state), İstanbul: Risale.

Faroqhi, Suraiya. 1987. *Men of Modest Substance: House Owners and House Property in Seventeenth-century Ankara and Kayseri,* Cambridge and New York: Cambridge University Press.

Fekete, L. 1965. "Taşralı Bir Türk Efendisinin Evi" (The House of a Provincial Turkish Gentleman), *Belleten* 116:615-38.

Findley, Carter. 1982. "The Acid Test of Ottomanism: The Acceptance of Non-Muslims in the Late Ottoman Bureaucracy." Vol. 1, pp. 339–68 in B. Braude and B. Lewis, eds. *Christians and Jews in the Ottoman Empire: The Functioning of a Plural Society.* New York: Holmes & Meier.

Foucault, Michel. 1977. *Discipline and Punish: The Birth of the Prison.* Translated by Alan Sheridan. New York: Pantheon Books.

Frangakis, Elena. 1985. "The Raya Communities of Smyrna in the 18th century." Pp. 27–42 in *Actes du Colloque Internationale d'Histoire. Le Ville Néohellénique. Héritages Ottomans et État Grec.* Athens: Bibliotheca.

Galante, Avram. 1985. *Histoire des juifs de turquie,* Vol. 1. İstanbul: İsis.

Gellner, Ernest. 1983. *Nations and Nationalism,* Oxford: Blackwell.

Gerber, Haim. 1982. "Jewish Tax Farmers in the Ottoman Empire in the 16th and 17th Centuries," *Journal of Turkish Studies* 10:143–55.

Gerber, Haim. 1982. "Le-toledot Ha-Yehudim Be-Kushta Be-Me'ot 17–18" (On the Jews of Constantinople in the 17th and 18th Centuries), *Pe'amim* 12:27–46.

Gerber, Haim. 1980. "Social and Economic Position of Women in an Ottoman City, Bursa, 1600–1700," *International Journal of Middle Eastern Studies* 12:231–44.

Goitein, S.D. 1970. "Minority Self-rule and Government Control in Early Islam," *Studia Islamica* 31:101–16.

Göçek, Fatma Müge. 1996. *Rise of the Bourgeoisie, Demise of Empire: Ottoman Westernization and Social Change,* New York: Oxford University Press.

Göyünç, Nejat. 1983. *Osmanlı İdaresinde Ermeniler* (Armenians in the Ottoman administration), İstanbul: Gültepe.

İnalcık, Halil. 1953. "15. Asır Türkiye İktisadî ve İçtimaî Tarihi Kaynakları" (Sources for Fifteenth-century Turkish Economic and Social History), *İstanbul Üni-*

versitesi İktisat Fakültesi Mecmuası 15/1-4: 51ï75.

İnalcık, Halil. 1991. "Ottoman Galata, 1453–1553." Pp. 17–116 in Edhem Eldem, ed. *Première rencontre internationale sur l'Empire ottoman et la Turquie moderne, recherches sur la ville ottomane: Le cas du quartier de Galata*, Istanbul and Paris: ISIS.

Issawi, Charles. 1982. "The Transformation in the Economic Position of Millets in the Nineteenth Century." Vol. 1, pp. 261–85 in B. Braude and B. Lewis, eds. *Christians and Jews in the Ottoman Empire: The Functioning of a Plural Society*. New York: Holmes & Meier.

Jennings, Ronald C. 1978. "Zimmis (Non-Muslims) in Early 17th Century Ottoman Judicial Records: The Sharia Court of Anatolian Kayseri," *Journal of the Economic and Social History of the Orient* 21:225–93.

Jennings, Ronald C. 1975. "Women in the Early 17th-century Ottoman Judicial Records: The Sharia Court of Anatolian Kayseri," *Journal of the Economic and Social History of the Orient* 28:53–114.

Karpat, Kemal. 1985. *Ottoman Population 1830–1914: Demographic and Social Characteristics*, Madison, Wis.: University of Wisconsin Press.

Kévorkian, Raymond H., and Paul B. Paboudjian, eds. 1992. *Les Arméniens dans l'Empire ottoman a la veille du génocide*, Paris: Éditions d'Art et d'Histoire ARHIS.

Lewis, Bernard. 1984. *The Jews of Islam*, Princeton: Princeton University Press.

Mandeville, Jon. 1966. "The Ottoman Courts of Syria and Jordan," *Journal of the American Oriental Society* 86:311–19.

Mantran, Robert. 1982. "Foreign Merchants and the Minorities in Istanbul During the Sixteenth and Seventeenth Centuries." Vol. 1, pp. 127–37 in B. Braude and B. Lewis, eds. *Christians and Jews in the Ottoman Empire: The Functioning of a Plural Society*. New York: Holmes & Meier.

Marcus, Abraham. 1983. "Men, Women and Property: Dealers in Real Estate in 18th Century Aleppo," *Journal of the Economic and Social History of the Orient* 26:137–63.

Nagata, Yuzo. 1976a. *Muhsinzade Mehmed Paşa ve Ayanlık Müessesesi* (The Institutions of Provincial Notables and Muhsinzade Mehmed Pasha), Tokyo: Institute for the Study of Languages and Cultures of Asia and Africa.

Nagata, Yuzo. 1976b. *Some Documents on the Big Farms of the Notables in Western Anatolia*, Tokyo: Institute for the Study of Languages and Cultures of Asia and Africa.

Ortaylı, İlber. 1989. "XVIII–XIX. Yüzyıllarda Galata" (Galata in the 18th and 19th centuries) in *Tarih Boyunca İstanbul Semineri*, İstanbul: İstanbul Üniversitesi Edebiyat Fakültesi Tarih Araştıma Merkezi.

Özkaya, Yücel. 1985. *Onsekizinci Yüzyılda Osmanlı Kurumları ve Osmanlı Toplum Yaşantaşı* (Ottoman Institutions and Ottoman Social Life in the Eighteenth Century), Ankara: Kültür ve Turizm Bakanlığı.

Papadopoullos, Theodore H. 1990. *Studies and Documents Relating to the History of the Greek Church and People under Turkish Domination*, Brookfield, Vt.: Gower.

Parkin, Frank. 1979. *Marxism and Class Theory: A Bourgeois Critique*, New York: Columbia University Press.

Parkin, Frank, ed. 1974. *The Social Analysis of Class Structure*, London: Tavistock.

Parkin, Frank. 1971. *Class Inequality and Political Order: Social Stratification in Capitalist and Communist Societies*, London: MacGibbon & Kee.

Rafeq, Abdulkarim. 1966. *The Province of Damascus, 1723–1783*, Beirut: Khayats.

Sarkiss, Harry Jewell. 1937. "The Armenian Renaissance, 1500–1863," *Journal of Modern History* 9/4:433–48.

Schacht, J. 1964. *An Introduction to Islamic Law*, Oxford: Clarendon Press.

Seng, Yvonne J. 1991. "The Üsküdar Estates (*Tereke*) as Records of Everyday Life in an Ottoman Town." Ph.D. dissertation, University of Chicago.

Smith, Anthony D. 1988. "The Myth of the 'Modern Nation' and the Myth of Nations," *Ethnic and Racial Studies* 11/1:1–26.

Smith, Anthony D. 1987. *The Ethnic Origins of Nations*, Oxford and New York: Blackwell.

Smith, Anthony D. 1983. *Theories of Nationalism*, New York: Holmes and Meier.

Steinsaltz, Adin. 1976. *The Essential Talmud*. Translated by Chaya Galai. New York: Basic Books.

Tucker, Judith. 1986. *Women in Nineteenth-century Egypt*, Cambridge: Cambridge University Press.

Üyepazarcı, Erol, ed. 1992. *İkinci Mahmut'un İstanbul'u: Bostancıbaşı Sicilleri* (The Istanbul of Mahmut II: The registers of the Bostancıbaşı), İstanbul: İstanbul Büyükşehir Belediyesi Kültür İşleri Dairesi Başkanlığı.

Uzunçarşılı, İsmail Hakkı. 1984. *Osmanlı Devletinin İlmiye Teşkilatı* (The organization of the ulema of the Ottoman state), Ankara: Türk Tarih Kurumu.

Veinstein, Giles. 1981. "Les Pelerins de la Mecque a travers quelques inventaires apres deces ottomans (XVIIe–XVIIIe siècles)," *Revue de l'Occident musulman et de la Méditerranée* 31:63–71.

Veinstein, Giles. 1979. "Trésor Public et Fortunes Privées dans l'Empire Ottoman (milieu XVI–debut XIX siècles," *Cahiers de la Méditerranée* 121–34.

Yazgan, Turan, ed. 1988. *Şer'iye Sicilleri: Mahiyeti, Toplu Kataloğu ve Seçme Hükümler* (Islamic law court records: Their character, union catalog, and selected decisions). Vol. 1. İstanbul: Türk Dünyası Araştırmaları Vakfı.

Notes

1. The term "minority" is used here with its sociological meaning; it denotes any social group that does not share equally in the resources of the society at large.

2. For instance, one specific study (Jennings 1978) on the court records in a seventeenth-century Anatolian city illustrates that non-Muslims accumulated land and buildings and, even though they did not engage in loan and credit to the same degree as Muslims, they nevertheless engaged in substantial interaction with Muslims and utilized the Islamic courts. For a more thorough discussion of the social location of minorities within Ottoman society, see Göçek 1996.

3. The great bulk of what has been written throughout history has been by and for elites. Literacy among non-elites has been commonplace only for a few hundred years in the West, and literate common people have infrequently left any record of their actions, relationships, or attitudes. Court records balance the historical accounts centering on the elite by providing material on the ordinary people.

4. The extent of use of the rules laid down in the Qur'an varies in practice (Schacht 1964: 76): its hold is strongest on the law of family, inheritance, and religious endowments, weakest on penal law, taxation, constitutional law, and law of war—with the law of contracts and obligations standing in the middle.

5. The extent of the judge's power and jurisdiction extended beyond matters of personal status such as marriage, divorce, inheritance, and child custody to include (Uzunçarşılı 1984: 134; Doumani 1985: 156–57) supervising and registering economic transactions, overseeing all religious institutions including endowments, overseeing trade, fixing prices of goods and transportation costs, controlling weights and measures, supervising the currency, adjudicating criminal and civil cases, overseeing poll-tax payments, endorsing heads of guilds, approving construction of new buildings and renovations. Hence the judge at once performed the functions of a legal executor, notary, and state official; he had to approve almost all societal transactions (Bayındır 1984).

6. The judges and the religious court did not have separate work quarters; they operated out of the house of the judge.

7. The archival inventory numbers of these three registers were, consecutively, 14/268, 14/395, and 14/493.

8. I would like to thank Ehud Toledano for alerting me to this possibility.

9. This observation is taken from a personal conversation with Bernard Lewis, June 1994.

10. An Ottoman census of 1850 estimated the Armenian artisans in Constantinople at 35,979, with 32,999 master and regular apprentices (Artinian 1989: 9).

Christian Communities in Eighteenth- and Early Nineteenth-century Ottoman Greece: Their Fiscal Functions

SOCRATES D. PETMEZAS

This paper has a double purpose. On the one hand, on a purely documentary level, I will collect and assess the existing aggregate data on local (communal and *kaza*[1]) finances in selected eighteenth-century Christian communities of Ottoman Greece. I will use this information, along with other available data on this subject, to elucidate the fiscal functions of the (rural and urban) territorial communities. On the other hand I will try to show that the evolution of the fiscal structure of these communities is part of a larger picture, i.e. this development can only be understood in the context of the transformation of Ottoman administrative and fiscal institutions in the late seventeenth and the eighteenth centuries. This transformation was the unintended result of decisions related to the amelioration of the imperial fiscal and administrative system, the new patterns of surplus distribution among competing sociopolitically dominant groups, and finally the emergence of a new powerful class of Christian "notables cum merchants-financiers," who benefited from the above transformations and enhanced their leading position in the Christian populations. Their domination of the communal institutions emerged as the most flexible means of power for these Christian notables in their effort to capture as large a part of the fiscal surplus as possible.

I must stress that I do not consider these transformations to be part of the long process of Ottoman imperial "decay" and of (Christian) national (-ist) "emergence." Recent studies have shown that it is certainly misleading to view the development of the Ottoman state and society in the seventeenth and eighteenth centuries as a linear process of political and societal decline, which is linked with the disarticulation of the "classical" administrative, military, and fiscal institutions and the decentralization of power in profit of the rapacious and malign groups of provincial notables, emerging big landowners, rebellious magnates, and the conquering new Judeo-Christian merchant and financier class.[2] The "decline" paradigm (in its multiple versions) was informed by an "essentialist" view of the Ottoman Empire in its "classical" sixteenth-century form, as a perfectly functional, centralized, and efficient (in a military and administrative sense) imperial state that ruled over a timorous and docile society, economically sophisticated but socially immune to any kind of internal dynamism.[3] Its supposedly innate cultural and social introversion (its "oriental stagnation") in an era of relentless military and economic competition with the expanding "West" inevitably led to a spiral of mutually reinforced processes of power decentralization, military decomposition, institutional disarticulation, societal dissolution, and economic underdevelopment. The inverse picture is of course the story of the subsequent effort of a dedicated small group of reformers to recentralize the empire, modernize its sociopolitical institutions, open its cultural and educational system to western influence, and finally help develop its economy. The national historiography of each of the nations (Turkish included) that once belonged to the Ottoman heartland has adopted this secular vulgate and included it in their own narration of events and sociopolitical processes inevitably leading to their own "national awakening" (or "regeneration"), which is in turn considered an integral part of a larger process of modernization and Westernization.

Contrary to the multiple variants of the decline paradigm, the novel approach sees the transformation of the Ottoman state and society in the seventeenth and eighteenth centuries as the result of internal demo-economic change, of meaningful ideological strife, of incessant conflict among social groups and political factions, and, finally, of the global process of competitive adaptation of the state structures to these societal mutations. No transcendental value is attached to this or the other processes of transformation, centralization, or modernization. This is not of course to deny that in the long period from the end of the sixteenth to the beginning of the nineteenth century the overall productivity and the technical sophistication of imperial economy grew less than those of most other European economies and that the process of intellectual and political emancipation of the European populations was unequalled by that of the Ottoman population, regardless of religion. The Ottoman case is one of unequal development and relative, not absolute, retardation and stagnation.

Territorial Communities and Communal Self-government in the Ottoman Heartland

The rural and urban Christian territorial communities have long since been viewed, by the national historiographies of the Balkan states, as the multivariate and informal yet functional and de facto recognized institutions "representing" the local Christian population. These institutions, which supposedly "blossomed under the relative freedom of the isolated mountains and the small arid islands," were thought to serve as the depositories of "popular" (and thus purely "national") customs, mores, and values. In nineteenth-century independent Greece, as in other Balkan countries, jurists influenced by the German historical school of law, in their effort to create and elaborate a national law system, sought its founding principles and inherently national forms in the communal/popular customs which were "preserved" in written or oral form. Later, at the end of the nineteenth century, the political principles that guided—as many thought—the quintessentially national, popular, and "democratic" communal administration were opposed to the degenerate and corrupted forms of the liberal parliamentary system, which was "imported" from Western Europe (i.e. foreign) and unduly imposed as a straitjacket on the national community. The study of the principles governing and the forms taken by "communal self-government" and the modalities and the limits of "communal autonomy" is, consequently, an area of research that resembles an ideological minefield and demands that the scholar exert the utmost prudence.

A terminological clarification is needed here. The word *koinotita* in Greek means indiscriminately commune and community. Hereafter I will use the word "community" to refer to the territorially defined group of people (rural or urban inhabitants) that is founded on the collective right of access to certain natural resources (arable, waste, pasture, and forest lands and water resources). I will reserve the word "commune" (and the modifier "communal") as a term describing the communities (of whatever size) which regularly chose some of their members as officials in charge of common fiscal, administrative, and, possibly, juridical affairs. State authorities made good use of these local institutions, either formally or informally, especially when these institutions offered unmatched help in the rapid and efficient collection of taxes, provided specialized valuable goods and services, or secured the political and military control of strategic places and communication axes. The collective fiscal responsibility of the rural and urban community was the cornerstone of the imperial fiscal system and the principal reason why the representative communal institutions were either tolerated or informally recognized.[4] Furthermore, the collective responsibility of the territorial community was extended in affairs of criminal justice and public order.

In the Ottoman heartland the principle of confessional segmentation of the population in religiously defined groups gave exceptional secular (juridical and administrative) power to the respective religious authorities. Consequently, the proper function of shared communal institutions in multiconfessional communities was made almost impossible.[5] This was a formidable obstacle to the proper development and consolidation of these institutions outside those territorial communities where only one confessional group predominated. The recognition of (informal) communal representation in the Ottoman Empire never encompassed a whole territorial community in perpetuity, treating it as an entity.[6] Of course, imperial edicts and orders were issued that granted specific fiscal, commercial, and administrative privileges to certain territorial communities[7] or to their constituent religious and professional groups. These should not be compared to communal charters granted by Western pre-modern states. Ottoman administrative practice fragmented the social sphere and its agents along religious, corporate, and professional lines, while any privilege bound only the sultan who granted it.

Islamic law recognized only real and not moral (or corporate) persons. Consequently, the "communal" officials and their charges were not recognized officially by the central and provincial Ottoman authorities but they were, nevertheless, used by the latter to facilitate certain fiscal and administrative tasks and they even tacitly and effectively represented the population of their community vis-à-vis the State officials. In the Islamic courts of law this informal recognition was effectuated by the legal stratagem of the presence of a group of (named or unnamed) individuals.[8] Tax-farmers and provincial magnates, for their part, co-operated with the chosen representatives of the territorial communities and they even gave a quasi-official form to this cooperation. Effectively, local notables, both Muslim *ayan* and Christian *kocabaşıs*, were those who, in spite of the fact that they were not included in the dominant office-bearing state elite (*rical*), could better and most efficiently assess and control the fiscal revenue sources in their respective areas.[9]

If we leave aside the legal-institutional formalism, we must underline that since the Ottoman state was reluctant to integrate officially the local Muslim (and Christian) notables into the office-bearing state elite, the informality of this relationship was of mutual interest. In the seventeenth and eighteenth centuries, the local notables were granted political privileges and access to economic and social power resources that they were usually not entitled to, while the central state elite did not suffer any loss of symbolic power and legitimacy or any severe curtailment of fiscal income. A modus vivendi was found to accommodate the provincial notables and the central state elite. This was founded on mutual interest concerning the collection and redistribution of fiscal income.[10]

The scanty evidence of the fiscal and administrative functions
of Christian communes in the early Ottoman centuries

We possess very little information about the communal institutions in the early Ottoman Balkans. During the first *istimalet*[11] phase of conquest, local urban-communal "autonomy" was tolerated and even officially recognized by the Ottoman state. Once Ottoman power was firmly established, the regular administrative system was imposed and did away with formal communal autonomy.[12] In the "classical age" (fifteenth to early seventeenth centuries), the *timar* system provided for the effective local presence of Ottoman officials, who assumed most of the necessary administrative and fiscal functions, like the repartition of fiscal dues, the assessment of individual fiscal obligations, and finally the collection and transfer of taxes.[13] The cooperation of village elders (*gerontes*) or urban parish headmen (*epitropoi*) was sought during the original registration and all the subsequent corrections of the provincial *tahrir* (survey) registers.[14] The engagement of local people in fiscal (and administrative) affairs was minimal and auxiliary. This does not mean that informal representative institutions in the Christian communities were totally extinct. They occasionally took part in fiscal and administrative operations and they certainly guaranteed the collective tax responsibility of the community. In most court documents that refer to border, pasture, or water disputes between villages, groups of villagers are enumerated, often assisting their Ottoman overlord (*sipahi, emin,* or *vakıf mütevveli*) as defendants or plaintiffs.[15] Furthermore, every community held in common economically significant natural resources or other items of property, protected them, regulated the access to these natural resources and, eventually, managed their mercantile exploitation.[16]

For the early centuries, we possess more detailed and precise information on urban communities, like Serres where a *protogeros* (chief elder) was attested since the fifteenth century. In the early seventeenth century a *protogeros* was still the head of the twelve-member secular council of the separate Christian community. Nevertheless, in Serres, as in all diocesan capitals, the bishop was the unquestioned spiritual and administrative authority of the Greek-Orthodox community, whose diocesan officialdom (along with the richer guild officials) formed the apex of the Christian society.[17] The bishop's court held significant juridical prerogatives on matters of family, civil, and even commercial law. Although bringing cases to the episcopal court was not obligatory for Christians, who could still bring cases to the *kadı*, it seems that in many cases the juridical power of the church was respected.[18] The officers of the guilds and the elders of rural villages and parishes had also relatively restricted judicial prerogatives, mostly as arbiters in minor intracommunal disputes. In the seventeenth-century example of the large and prosperous Macedonian multiconfessional town of Serres, a simple capital of *kaza*, the administration of the financial affairs of the Christian community was in the hands of a special committee manned with representatives of each important guild. The ecclesiastical, communal, and guild organizations were manned and governed by men like Synadinos, who was a guild officer, a parish vicar and a member of the local diocesan officialdom (*sakkelarios*). We have clear evidence that in the first half of the seventeenth century a group of local notables, both Christian *kocabaşıs* and Muslim *ayan*, participated informally in the governance of local fiscal and administrative affairs.[19] In this same town, the fundamental cellular corporate entity was the parish neighborhood (*mahalle*), administered by its vicar, who was assisted by parish headmen (*epitropoi*). In the early centuries of Ottoman rule, priests and clerical officials were among the richer and socially most prominent members of the Christian communities and were particularly visible in communal representation.[20] They administered the common parish property, whose income provided for the subsistence needs and financial assistance of the poor and the community at large. The same phenomenon was observed in late-eighteenth-century Athens, where parish councils still provided the basic services of social welfare and fulfilled a function of social discipline.[21] Consequently, in the urban communities the ecclesiastical organization, the professional guilds, and the parish neighborhoods formed a nexus of formal institutions that legally or informally represented the Greek Orthodox Christian population, managed its common property, and provided a modicum of self-government of common affairs. In the much smaller, and socially undifferentiated, rural communities such a diversification of functions between communal, professional, and ecclesiastical institutions was ineffectual; the parish and the communal representation were identical.

Social stratification and moral economy

The village and urban communities were conservative institutions founded on (and in their turn preserving) the rules and values of a "moral economy," which provided for the social and economic reproduction of local societies in general, and of individual households in particular. These rules and values were partly incorporated in the Ottoman *kanunname*s (Codes of Laws)[22] or in the infinite variety of local codification of the ecclesiastic, civil, and family legislation dispensed by the church (*nomokanones*).[23] Most of these values guaranteed that the principle of collective responsibility on fiscal and criminal affairs would be upheld without exerting disproportionate pressure on a minority of the community's population. Consequently, in order to assure that a sustainable relation between the number of taxpayers and the global taxation was maintained and that no household was ruined from over-taxation[24] or farm fragmentation,[25] the community regulated the movement of human resources and the use and transfer of productive resources (both those collectively and individually held). The community also fostered a sense of introversion and imposed a system of internal regulations that minimized the intervention of state authorities and isolated the latter from communal affairs.[26] Rural and urban communities built internal consensus by alleviating the fiscal and economic pressure on poorer households, through the meticulous conservation of all the egalitarian rights of use on commonly held natural resources, and through the maintenance of collective rights of use on individual properties (i.e. obligatory crop rotation, common grazing in the fallow, etc.). These collective constraints on the use of individual property were to the advantage of the poorer households. The same is true for the rules that regulated economic activity in periodic markets and which stipulated that no "stranger" (i.e. merchant) could buy the items for sale before a certain hour of the day, thus guaranteeing the provision of poorer members of the community with the necessary foodstuffs and raw materials.[27]

In small and poor villages and small towns the social differentiation of the population was relatively restrained, which does not mean that social inequality was inconsequential or that there were no barriers between social groups.[29] We have a pretty good picture of the inequalities in land tenure in many Greek villages and small townships in the seventeenth and especially in the eighteenth century, as pictured through the communal registers that assessed agricultural taxation. It is true that in the Greek cases these were predominantly small-owner insular communities, where a part of the population was seasonally employed in non-agricultural activities to supplement its household income.[30] Peasant farms were fragmented and the economy as a whole was deficient in cereal production. But local social predominance is founded on relative and not on absolute difference. The best description of the dense internal social stratification (and spatial variance) of a late-seventeenth-century insular agricultural economy is given in the example of Santorini,[31] where an important number of independent small-owners lived side by side with a small group of prosperous landowners and a large population of peasants, who either had insufficient land or were completely landless and had to supplement their household's revenue with salaried or extra-agricultural employment. A similar structure can be observed in the mid-nineteenth-century town of Zagora (see table 1). It is interesting to note that in the mid-nineteenth-century Bulgarian cases, in the agriculturally rich villages of the Koyuntepe *nahiyesi* (*sancak*[32] of Felibe) in 1841 and in the three *kaza*s of Ruse, Sumen, and Sliven in the 1860s, the agricultural taxation is more equally distributed, although local social inequality is, of course, the predominant fact.[33]

Table 1. Unequal distribution of agricultural taxation
in comparable nineteenth century Balkan cases[28]

Taxpayer groups*	Skyros island (1817)	Zagora (1836)	Zagora (ca. 1854)	Taxpayer groups*	Koyuntepe *nahiyesi* (1841)
0–20%	7.61%	1.03%	1.59%	0–25%	11%
21–40%	11.62%	4.87%	6.34%	26–50%	18%
41–60%	19.18%	10.99%	12.53%	51–75%	25%
61–80%	22.50%	23.40%	22.95%	76–100%	45%
81–100%	39.09%	59.71%	56.59%		
Total	100%	100%	100%		100%
Gini coefficient		0.526	0.524		

*The taxpayers are classified according to their financial obligation,
in four or five groups of equal size in ascending order of "fiscal wealth."

The culmination of communal self-government in the eighteenth and early nineteenth centuries

Fiscal and administrative transformations

In the seventeenth and, increasingly, in the eighteenth century, the Ottoman administrative and fiscal system underwent a series of structural transformations that changed completely the relations between the taxpayers (grouped in collectively taxed communities) and the Ottoman authorities. A series of new taxes, levies, and dues (like the *avarız-ı divaniyye* and the *tekâlif-i örfiyye*)[34] were demanded as a global fiscal obligation from each administrative division. The global sum (and the additional expenses for its collection) was allotted to the subaltern administrative levels (i.e. *kaza*) according to a previously negotiated (or newly re-negotiated) repartition (*tevzi*) matrix. The slow dissolution of the *timar* system (and its substitution by the *mukataa* system)[35] gradually deprived the Ottoman fiscal authorities of the assistance of locally based Ottoman officials, both knowledgeable of the local situation (i.e. capable of rightly assessing individual fiscal capacity) and able to exert effective pressure on recalcitrant taxpayers. At the same time, this dissolution greatly expanded the aggregated sum of taxes effectively collected in cash, since the fiscal dues directly paid to the *sipahi* were now in part transferred to the imperial treasury. The *kadı* and the local Muslim and non-Muslim notables took upon themselves the task of negotiating the repartition matrix, of assessing the fiscal capacity at every administrative level (*kaza*, village or parish/*mahalle* community, and individual household) and finally of overseeing or effectuating the collection of taxes.[36] It is not surprising that this development coincides with the growth of disposable documentation in Greek on the fiscal and administrative functions of the Christian communities in the eighteenth century.[37]

Furthermore, the expansion of the *malikâne* (lifelong tax lease),[38] after the close of the seventeenth century, intensified the transformation of the Ottoman administrative and fiscal system. This transformation has recently been termed a process of "privatization" of fiscal resources and "provincialization" of administrative-fiscal power.[39] In this way local notables undertook the complicated, expensive, but vital tasks of social and financial control over the rural and urban population and hence became an integral part of the imperial fiscal, military, and administrative system. They were co-opted into the dominant classes—without ever becoming full members of the tax-free ruling elite—in a process that both enhanced the legitimacy of the Ottoman dynasty and provided new sources of military and financial power to the central treasury. The new *malikâne* tax leases were principally appropriated by members of the central elite (and their financial partners), but a significant part of them devolved to the local notables (*ayan* and *kocabaşı*s) and to the provincial magnates. It is especially *malikâne* leases of agricultural fiscal revenue sources (which required the close inspection of the beneficiary and produced lower profits) that were offered to local tax-farmers and subcontractors, while more lucrative commercial fiscal revenue sources were the appanages of the members of the central state elite. Lifelong leases (with an option of being offered to the beneficiary's heir) of regrouped fiscal sources were as close to private property as possible, and contemporaries treated them almost as that: "privatized" property. Close ties of political factionalism and economic interdependence were woven between households of the central elite and local notable families. Fiscal and administrative tasks and, consequently, real and effective political authority were delegated to the local notables, even though they might not have any officially recognized state authority. The process of "provincialization" (i.e. consolidation of "provincial autonomy" on matters of local administration, finances, public order, and security) was characteristic of the eighteenth century and served both the needs of the Ottoman state and the interests of the central-state elite, the provincial magnates and the local notables.

In the *mukataalu* lands, the tithes and the other taxes and dues that were registered as proportional to the estimated local agricultural production were often lumped in global dues to the treasury (*mal-i mirî*) or the tax-farmer and were consequently unrelated to the value of the agricultural production and thus to the taxpayers' income. In most of the documented cases of functioning communal institutions where the taxes paid by the communities are known, these communities are *vakıf* or *mukataalu* lands given in *iltizam* (short-term tax-farming) or in *malikâne*. Some of these tax units (*mukataa*) were sub-farmed to the communes themselves against lump sum payments (*mal-i maktu*).[40] It is interesting to observe that in the rare cases of *timarlı* lands, as in Zagorye *nahiyesi*, the tithe (called *kesim*) and the *ispence* (called *baştina*) paid to the *sipahi* are expressed in lump sums.[41] Otherwise the most important taxes besides the head tithe (*cizye*) and the sheep tax (*celep*) are the distributive taxes known as *avarız-ı divanıyye*, *tekâlif-i örfiye* and *tekâlif-i sakka*. At the end of the eighteenth century, new taxes, like the *resm-i zacriye* and the *resm-i mizan-ı harir*, were added, administered by the new financial departments of the *irade-i cedid* and the *tersane-i âmire-i hazinesi*. The consolidation of communal administration in eighteenth- and early nineteenth-century Greece is thus intimately related to the new forms of taxation: the distributive taxes and the lump sum assessment.

The local notables as the indispensable partners

The tax-farmers or the *emin*, who administered the *mukataalu* lands, were occasional visitors in the area and did not command the necessary knowledge or the prestige to evaluate rightly the fiscal capacity of each community and to assess individually the household's income. They were thus obliged to look for the necessary partners and found them in the local notables. Only the latter had the knowledge to assess correctly the taxable capacity of every individual household and to mobilize the social consensus for the swift payment of dues in cash, in kind, and in labor without unnecessary friction.

Without their assistance, tax-collection would be effectuated mainly through physical threat and violence and thus destabilize the social hierarchies in the local communities, undermine the legitimacy of Ottoman rule, and most probably bias the allocation of economic resources and wear out the fiscal revenue source itself.[42] In other words, the use of communal notables as *fiscal* intermediaries reduced the overhead cost of tax collection and provided an economically more neutral mode of tax assessment and collection.

It is necessary here to examine the economic and social foundations of the power of the *kocabaşı*s in the Christian communities. In agricultural societies land is not solely an economic resource; it is the most valued symbolic marker of personal respectability and familial prestige. It is not surprising that the *kocabaşı*s did not seek landed property as a source of income only, but also as the foundation of social excellence. They were thus both the most prominent landowners and household heads (*noikokyrides*) and the unanimously recognized exemplary figures of communal leadership (*prokritoi*). They were also those who as grocers, merchants, and manufacturers dominated the non-agricultural sectors of the local (and sometimes the regional) economy and who held together the local credit network. Possessing the largest part of locally disposable cash and other financial assets, they were indispensable for providing loans to other members of the community or for lending the necessary cash to the community.[43] The merchants and the notables of the largest towns in every district, being in the lead of competing networks of local alliances, exercised a prominent role in the social and economic affairs of their region. It was usual that a *kocabaşı*, or a group of notables, simply represented the community and on its behalf auctioned its own fiscal dues expressed in lump sums (*ber vech-i maktu*).[44] In such cases the *kocabaşı*s, in their position as political intermediaries between the Ottoman state and the communal corporate body, were held personally responsible for the collection and payment of the farmed taxes, as they were usually representing their commune as principal guarantors (*kefil*) of its debt.[45] This is the reason why the Christian merchants and financiers in large towns, where they felt secure enough to disregard the value of community as a protective shield, were reluctant to engage capital (and their time) in non-commercial activities (i.e. in low-interest credit to the commune) or in risky engagements (i.e. serving as guarantors for the Christian community).[46] Of course, lending money to individuals or to corporate bodies was not a gratuitous act and entailed some very important advantages to the lender. On a personal and purely economic basis, merchant activities were facilitated when a large number of small-scale producers felt morally or financially obliged to turn to their lender as the natural buyer of their excess production. This kind of personal bond could be transformed to a more stable personal relation (described as "economic paternalism"), whereby the *kocabaşı*—as a lenient lender and a generous buyer—formed a malleable group of loyal local supporters of his political endeavors. When a *kocabaşı* had the opportunity to assess and collect taxes, this kind of personal economic-cum-political relationship between him and a large part of his fellow townsfolk was intensified. Consequently, the notables in many communities strove to dominate and, if possible, to monopolize both the local credit market and the communal political sphere.

The richer and more powerful notables could offer the necessary cash in order to cover unpredictable and large communal expenses, to assure protection of the commune by influential powerbrokers in Istanbul or in the provincial capital, and finally, reaching the apex of social prominence and economic power, to sub-farm the local taxes. In the third case, they started to dissociate themselves from the corporate body of the Christian community and took the position of the fiscal overlord. Once securely installed as communal treasurers and tax-farmers, *kocabaşı*s might be tempted to profit from this strategic position. But the local sociopolitical system was one of competitive politics between factions of more or less equal strength, and this monopolization of power could only be of short duration. Alliances were bound to dissolve, the Ottoman protectors themselves were insecure of their position, and reversal of position and "fate" was the most natural outcome. When powerful *sadrazam*s and palace favorites fell from power or died, their protégés immediately followed them in fall, exile, or death.

Local power politics were an exercise in intrigue and survival, which curiously enough meant moderation and a striving for consensual decision-making. A moderate administration would neither disregard the interests of poorer households, nor radically exclude any opposing *kocabaşı* faction from the distribution of fiscal surplus, vital decision-making, and the other privileges related to communal administration. This would promote internal communal cohesion, but it would also undermine the cohesion of each faction and thus it would make realignment of intracommunal political alliances easier, promoting, consequently, intrigue and disloyalty. On the contrary, any effort by *kocabaşı*s to permanently monopolize communal leadership and its profits might strengthen factional loyalty, but these cases of rigid factional politics would certainly end in one of two ways: the opposing *kocabaşı* faction would either adopt class alignment as a novel discourse and a practice of mobilization, thus undermining the internal cohesion of the commune,[47] or invite the interference of external power groups (*ayan*, provincial magnates, church authorities)[48] with the same destabilizing effect. Nevertheless, these were real but extreme cases. Consequently, parallel to their conscious effort to profit individually from their position as financial and political mediators, the *kocabaşı*s' principal (but not only) concern was to secure the reproduction of the institutional and socioeconomic foundations of their power, i.e. the community of independent small cultivators.

Cooperation and competition between Christian and Muslim provincial notables

The monopolization of information on local conditions and of the (informal) representation of their communities opened for the *ayan* and *kocabaşı*s large political, social, and economic possibilities. Hence the structural resemblance of *ayan* and *kocabaşı*s was reinforced by mutual cooperation in provincial and local factional politics.[49] There existed nevertheless a fundamental and decisive difference between the two groups. The Muslim *ayan* could use his position in local and provincial administration as a first step in a career of upward social mobility toward a state office and toward his incorporation into the central state elite. Then the *ayan*-turned-*paşa* could choose to dissociate himself and his household from his local "constituents," although many provincial magnates had striven to keep in touch with their local friends and "clients." For the Christian *kocabaşı*s no such outlet was open, even though they had been routinely (and rightfully) accused of maltreating their fellow Christians and of profiting from the administration of communal finances.

Thus the principal opponents and competitors of the Christian *kocabaşı*s were none other than the Muslim provincial magnates and the powerful *ayan*, who would profit from fiscal over-exploitation, financial stringency, and communal indebtedness in order to expropriate common (and individual) peasant properties and transform the communities of independent small-owners into a quasi-private large estate (*çiftlik*). The usual method adopted by prospective *çiftlik sahipleri* to force the expropriation of communal and peasant land was to secure the ability to impose, assess, and collect taxes; to monopolize the high-interest credit market to which the indebted community was turning; and to control the local militia who protected the area from brigands, while at the same time acting as such.[50] Once a community was transformed into a *çiftlik*, the surplus produced was in priority captured by the new landlord to the disadvantage of both rich *kocabaşı*s and poor peasants. This kind of competition for the surplus distribution between the Christian communal notables, on the one hand, and a host of Muslim provincial magnates and *ayan*, on the other hand, was a permanent feature of the eighteenth and early nineteenth centuries. When political-military power, fiscal control, and credit dominance were concentrated on one side, the outcome was usually the expropriation of the individual and communal property.

The Christian *kocabaşı*s thus faced the following dilemma: close cooperation with the *ayan* and/or tax-farmers might guarantee them high profits in the short term, but in the long term they would probably undermine the internal coherence of their community and destroy the foundation of their social, economic, and political power: the independent communal institutions that they dominated. To face that threat they were obliged to exert self-restraint and refrain from using their economic and financial power to their full extent. Until the Tanzimat reform period (1839–41), no case of a Christian expropriating peasant and common properties and of forming large land estates is observed. The landed property of Panayotis Benakis, a powerful and rich *kocabaşı*, was constituted by a large number of small land parcels dispersed over a large area.[51] Instead of using their credit-market power to expropriate the small peasants, they were more inclined to weave relations of interdependence, exerting with profit the power of economic paternalism.

Communal Fiscal Management in Its Maturity: Quantitative Examples (Late Eighteenth–Early Nineteenth Century)

The development and consolidation of the fiscal and administrative functions of the Christian communities since the late seventeenth century is consequently closely related, on the one hand, to the structural societal transformations of the Ottoman empire, which gave more power to the provincial magnates and notables, and, on the other hand, to the incessant competition of Christian and Muslim notables and tax-farmers in their effort to dominate the local societies and seize the largest possible portion of locally produced economic surplus. Only the richest and most prominent *kocabaşı*s in areas particularly privileged (by economic prosperity, historical circumstances, or geographic position) could successfully compete against the *ayan* and the powerful provincial magnates. Their success was closely linked to the rise and elaboration of communal institutions. It is difficult—and probably mis- leading and useless—to establish either a neat evolutionary pattern for the development of small Christian territorial communities towards a fully "self- governed commune" or a comprehensive typology of all the different forms which communities subjected in such a process can take. It is certainly easier to examine historically concrete examples of communities that have devel- oped in various degrees their own internal fiscal, financial, and "governing" institutions and bodies. This is what I propose to do in the rest of this study. A number of cases will be used to illustrate various configurations of state, *ayan,* and communal interaction, cooperation, and conflict. Some notes on the particular time and place setting will be given when necessary.

A First Case Study: The Small Proto-industrial Town of Zagora

In the second half of the eighteenth century the almost exclusively Chris- tian communities on Mount Pelion in eastern Thessaly, already involved in silk raising since the seventeenth century, experienced an unprecedented prosperity thanks to the development of proto-industrial production.[52] They were divided into two groups: the group of fourteen communities known as *vakıflı* that comprised the Argalast Mukataası,[53] whose revenues formed part of the Haremeyn Vakfı revenues, controlled by the administration of the imperial harem; and the group of the other ten communities known as *haneli,* which were annexed to various *has* possessions. In the final decades of the eighteenth century, Zagora, with a Greek Orthodox population of 500–800 households, was the largest and richest of seven eastern Pelion localities (villages and small townships), which specialized in silkworm breeding, the production of coarse woollen stuff (called *skouti*) and its itinerant fabrication into woollen cloth (called *kapota*). Rich merchant-financiers, residing in the area and in Constantinople, financed these protoindustrial activities, which involved the temporary emigration of fabricants to the final consumption areas. These merchants were themselves members of the prestigious local *kocabaşı* families. Zagora and its neighboring localities did not constitute the only proto-industrial network in Pelion. Some villages and small townships of the western slope of Pelion were themselves prosperous centers of silkworm breeding, cotton dyeing, and mixed (silk and cotton *alaca*) stuff weaving. All villages specialized in silkworm breeding and commercial export agriculture (olive oil, wine, and fruits) and the mountainous Pelion region itself was densely populated. A lively intellectual progress accompanied the socioeconomic development of this protoindustrial nexus in the second half of the eighteenth century. Undoubtedly the rational registration of all matters related to communal finances and the sophistication in the communal accounting techniques was influenced by this intellectual florescence.

The complex system of communal financial registers and archives

The small rural township of Zagora, standing at an altitude of 500 meters on the northeastern slopes of Mount Pelion, can be used to illustrate the full development of *internal* fiscal and financial institutions.[54] The Zagora Library possesses the almost complete series of its balance sheets for the years 1783–1822.[55] All revenues and expenses (starting at June 1) are neatly kept for every fiscal year along with a complete list of all creditors (registered every year on September 1). These balance sheets and creditors' lists give us abundant detail about the fiscal and financial functions of this particular community. An elected or co-opted member of the communal council acted as chief treasurer (*sakkoula*) and kept in check all accounts. He was probably assisted by the salaried secretaries (*grammatikoi*) of all five parishes of the township. He prepared and officially presented every year a balance sheet where all revenues and expenses were itemized. It is certain that an accounting journal was used where all daily transactions were kept and later aggregated to calculate the specific items that appear in the annual balance sheet. He must have also kept a ledger for the debts contracted by the community on an annual or monthly level. This ledger must have been used to pay the "bondholders" their interest and to prepare the list of creditors presented every year. Separate registers were kept to help him assess the tax contribution of each household. One of them was the register of all the male population (called *haratzodefteron* i.e. *haraç defteri*), which was used to assess the *cizye* contribution of every individual member of the community. Another account register was used to keep track of *cizye* collection and payment to the relevant Ottoman officer (*cizyedar*). Arrears of *cizye* payments were included in this register. Until the financial year 1793/94, the *cizye*, both the aggregate sum collected from contributors and the instalments paid to the *cizyedar*, were included respectively in the revenues and the expenses of the annual balance sheet. From June 1794 only the net profit or loss of the separate *cizye* account figured in the annual balance sheet.[56]

In a rural or urban community, where the communal officers had the authority to assess and collect taxes, one of their most important tasks was to evaluate, according to their own "internal" criteria, the "fiscal capacity" of every household. In Zagora this was done in a detailed and formal way. In every parish "estimators" were chosen to assess and register the agricultural property of every household.[57] In this register, called *mana* in Pelion, every individual source of agricultural revenue (vineyards, chestnuts, mulberries, olives, and all other productive trees, beehives, and goats) was registered, parcel after parcel. For every individual source of revenue, in every parcel, the appointed estimators evaluated its productivity (in physical terms) and its expected fiscal value. The aggregated fiscal value of the revenue of every household's agricultural property was thus calculated and could be used to allocate taxes. Every transfer of property (sale, dowry, ante-mortem donation or post-mortem inheritance) was registered and thus the real fiscal capacity of the concerned households was adequately corrected. Every few years the operation of official estimation and subsequent registration of agricultural properties was repeated. The secretaries of each parish were responsible for producing and updating this valuable cadastre.

It is thus evident that an efficient and well-informed group of local officials kept detailed registers and controlled the communal finances. These registers, originally intended for tax allotment, were used by the community for other reasons as well. The *mana*, for instance, was a cadastre that registered almost all the agricultural properties and their devolution. Any property litigation in the community could be solved using this register.

The foundation of communal independence and *kocabaşı* domination

This rational administrative and financial structure was the result of two converging processes that developed in a period when the local society experienced unprecedented economic prosperity and intellectual florescence (ca. 1750–1821):

1. The emergence and consolidation of a powerful group of communal notables, who were important landowners (compared to other members of the local Christian society), merchants and financiers, controlling the commercial exchanges (export of silk and olive oil and import of the necessary foodstuffs) and the proto-industrial activities in eastern Pelion and the various *loci* of itinerant fabrication of woollen cloth.[58]

2. The growing communal control over the taxation system, which ended with the almost complete "isolation" of the individual members of the community from the Ottoman tax collectors. The communal financial administration took in charge all the relevant functions and role of the tax collector and of the taxpayer. Thus two separate fiscal-financial systems, one "external" and one "internal," coexisted. The distinction between the two systems will be discussed in the next section.

It is to this second process that we will now turn our attention. Information is available from 1754, but of course it is only starting in 1783 that we can observe in detail the form locally taken by taxation. We shall begin by concentrating on the emergence of a flexible local credit market, which was mainly financed by local notables and led gradually to the substitution of the former Muslim and Jewish creditors by local Christians.

Debt amortization

We know that on March 1, 1754, the community of Zagora was indebted for 69,835 *guruş* and 60 *akçe* to Muslims and Jews.[59] The first group held 54% of the total amount. The money was owned mainly to Abdeddin Bey and Mustafa Bey, "lords" of Zagora (*afendes mas*), and to Mehmed Ağa, the *harem kethüdası*.[60] Other Muslims like Yusuf *Hazinedar Ağa* held smaller shares. Interest was as high as 15%, in an era of slow devaluation of the silver *guruş*.[61] Three Jewish financiers, Joseph Sarrafoglu, Bohor and Isaac Sitoglu, held the remaining 46% of the total sum and the interest paid to them was as high as 20%. A substantial part (10%) of the debt was due to the capitalization of unpaid interest. It is also evident that in 1754 a new loan of 19,553 *guruş* was borrowed from the Jewish bankers to pay the year's taxes (*mal-i maktu, kara astar, iştira,* and *harc-ı vilayet*[62]) and other unspecified expenses. The debt of the previous year (1753), which is evaluated at 43,414 *guruş,* soared in one year by 61%. If we compare this debt with total communal expenses of the year 1783/84 (22,533 *guruş*), we must admit that in 1754 the accumulated debt (*borc-ı mukaddem*) was probably three times the sum of current expenses.[63]

This could have resulted in the classical spiral of collective indebtedness and peasant land expropriation so often described in the relevant literature. But it seems that the threat of financial destabilization and communal alienation was avoided, thanks to the strong financial position of the communal notables and the efficient use of the privileges (which were by no means exceptional) extended to the community by the Sublime Porte. For the period up to 1783, information is rare and the only quantitative data concern the amortization of this heavy collective debt in the years 1761–79. Almost every year the communal notables paid a part of the debt to their Muslim and Jewish creditors.[64] This debt owed to people foreign to the commune I shall name "external debt." To amortize their "external" debt, communal notables had to borrow money from rich and not-so-rich members of the community, contracting thus what I shall name the "internal debt." In June 1784, Zagora owed 35,010 *guruş,* of which only 8,800 were owed to Jews and Muslims. In the following years this tendency would be confirmed. The communal debt would soar to finance unexpected expenses, but it would be mostly covered by community members who offered a much lower interest rate (6–10%). This "internal" debt would become a functional part of the local economy, providing a steady income to small bondholders, local funds, and endowments.[65]

Enhancing communal independence: financing armed militias, obtaining fiscal-administrative privileges, and securing powerful protectors

The solid financial position of its notables and their policy of attachment to powerful protectors had helped Zagora to isolate itself from the regular fiscal environment. A note in the communal register, dated in May 1765, enumerated twenty-eight different imperial edicts that were preserved in the communal safe-box (*sendik*).[66] Many of them referred to border litigation with neighboring communities, but some of them were of primary importance. They proclaimed that most taxes were to be paid in lump sums (*maktu*) and that all provincial authorities (*paşas* or *voyvodas*) were expressly forbidden to extract money during their visits to the community (*tayin*).

It should be added to the above that Zagora, like all the other Pelion localities, was not subjected to the authority of the Volos *kadı*, but was annexed to the distant *kaza* of Izdin (present day Lamia). The control exerted by the Ottoman juridical authorities was thus minimized. The communal authorities undertook a large part of the *kadı*'s legal and fiscal prerogatives (securing public order and collecting the windfall revenues of *bad-ı hava* and *cürm ve ceremeyn*) against a modest annual levy paid to the *kadı*. Furthermore it seems that Zagora, without being a part of the Argalast Mukataası, enjoyed many of its privileges. It is evident that the communal notables of Zagora, like those of other Pelion communities,[67] had consciously tried to identify themselves with the *vakıf*. In fact, in 1798/99 the community succeeded in putting itself under the protection of Hadice Sultan (1766–1822), sister of Sultan Selim III, and from that time it regularly paid a "gift" (*pişkeş*) to her and to her *kethuda*.

Debt amortization and protection from far-off protectors would have been of little help if Zagora and the other Christian communities in eastern Thessaly had not been able to protect themselves. To achieve that, they used their assets (economic power and powerful protectors) to ensure that a loyal Christian armed militia (*derbentçi* or *martolos*) was formed, in the 1770s, and that it was strong enough to resist the groups of bandits and competing *ayan* militias. Time and again the strong local militia kept Albanian bandits in check. In this way the Pelion *koçabaşıs* managed to secure public order in their territory and to actively exert a limited but real administrative and juridical power.

The combination of two distinctive fiscal echelons: "external" and "internal"

The study of the annual accounts of Zagora for the fiscal years 1783/84–1821/22 can reveal the basic characteristics of the communal financial system. There were two separate sides or echelons in the fiscal mechanism of the community: one "external," which dealt with the fiscal demands of the

Figure 1. Annual balance sheet and accumulated debt of Zagora in
current and constant *guruş* (*cizye* estimation included since 1794)

superior administrative authorities and followed the regulations of the standard Ottoman taxation system, and one "internal," which dealt with the contributions of members of the community and was controlled and regulated
according to communal rules and criteria. To a large extend, the "external"
echelon coincided with the expenses while the "internal" echelon was identified with the revenues of the community.

- Every year the community paid to the various Ottoman overlords
  a number of ordinary taxes and other personal levies, most of them
  in lump sums (*maktuat*). It also met unexpected extraordinary contributions and taxes, sent gifts (*pişkeş*) to its protectors in Constantinople, paid for the expenses of the local militia and the communal
  administration, serviced its communal debt, etc.

- The chief treasurer and the five parish secretaries collected from
  each household their specific fiscal contributions that were totally
  unrelated to the standard Ottoman taxation. The *cizye* was the only

exception. The community collected or assisted in the collection of the head tithe using its own registers. Otherwise the commune had organized its own "internal" levies, based on the evaluation of agricultural property, silk and maize production, etc. The poorer members of the community were allowed to postpone the payment of their current contribution. These arrears (a short-term credit, extended from the commune to its needy members) were reported (and usually collected) in the accounts of the subsequent year.

- In order to meet an unexpected rise in the annual expenses, the treasurer borrowed money, usually from the "internal" market (i.e. from other members of the community). In years of low expenses he looked after the rapid amortization of the "external" debt and the substitution of high-interest-bearing bonds with lower-interest-bearing bonds. He balanced his accounts every year with a profit or loss reported in the next year's financial use.

In effect, in the last forty years before the Greek War of Independence (1783/84–1821/22), Zagora paid a host of well-defined ordinary taxes[68] like the *mal-i maktu*,[69] the *cizye*, the *kara astar*,[70] the *iştira*,[71] the *resm-i zacriye*,[72] the *bedel-i harir*,[73] the *harc-ı vilayet*,[74] and the *umur-i şeri*[75] (see table 2). There were also some other contributions and gifts regularly paid to the "protectors" of the community, like the *pişkeş* to its "lord"[76] or to Hadice Sultan,[77] or the expenses for the *amillik*[78] and the salaries (*ulûfe*) of the *derbentçi*s and other armed guards.[79] Other local expenses were providing for the ecclesiastical taxes, the maintenance of schools and roads, and the salaries of local officials. The aggregate sum of these ordinary and regular expenses was easily predictable. It was generously covered by the annual revenues of the community, which were the following: the collection of *cizye* (according to unspecified criteria),[80] the annual contribution of each household according to its agricultural property (assessed using the *mana* register),[81] along with some tithes (silk, maize) paid only by those producing these articles. The communal accounts were balanced with a small profit or loss (*saldos*), which was reported (without interest) as an article of revenues or expenses respectively to the next year's financial use.[82] The occasional small loss was probably covered with a short-term loan advanced by the treasurer.

Table 2. The ordinary taxes of the town of Zagora (1783/84–1821/22)

Taxes	Period	Net sum in guruş	Additional expenses	Type of tax-farm and recipient	Makt?
Mal-i maktu	1754–1799	3,750	21.5%	Malikâne	Yes
	1800–1808	4,000	2.5%	Maktu iltizam	Yes
	1809–1822	7,500	7.8%	Malikâne, Velyuddin Paşa (Larissa valisi)	Yes
Kara astar	1784–1808	1,666.5 (1,666 guruş 20 para)	4.6%	Astarcı	Yes
	1808–1822	1,771	5.5%		Yes
Resm-i zacriye	1793–1795	850	33.6%	İrade-i cedid	Yes
	1796	1,000	19.6%		
	1797–1798	1,250	11.1%		
	1799–1810	2,000	5.6%		
	1811–1822	2,200	2.9%		
Bedeat-i harir	1810–1822			Tersane-i âmire (deruhde to Velyuddin Paşa?)	No
Harc-ı vilayet	1784–1804	500	1.6%	Larissa valisi	Yes
	1805–1822	1,200	2.1%		Yes
Umur-i şeri	1784–1822	260	16.5%	Izdin kadısı	Yes
İştira	1811–1822			Velyuddin Paşa (Larissa valisi)	No
Pişkeş	1789–1816			Abdeddin Beğ (Larissa)	No
Various pişkeş	1801–1809	1,300		Sultan hanım and other harem officials	Yes

Profiting from High Inflation

From 1770, after a period of relative stability that began early in the eighteenth century, the Ottoman silver guruş experienced a long-term decrease of its purchasing power, which is reflected in the exponential rise of prices, wages, and taxes. This inflation is the concurrent result of the debasement of the currency and the depreciation of silver relative to gold. Nominal taxation, which in our balance sheets is expressed in Ottoman guruş, was rapidly growing, both in Zagora and in other known cases. If the same sum is expressed in gold pieces, then it fluctuated around a slowly growing average (see figure 1). Given that lump-sum taxation and communal debt are expressed in silver coins, the community as a borrower and a taxpayer greatly profited from the exponential devaluation of the Ottoman silver guruş. The very slight long-term increase of real taxation was counterbalanced by the population growth in the same period.[83]

Table 3. The account balance, the debt, and the *guruş* deflator
(my own estimates in bold characters)

	guruş deflator (1770=1.0)	current *guruş*			constant *guruş*				debt variables		
		revenues	expenses	standing debt	revenues	expenses	loss and profit	standing debt	debt / balance	no. of creditors	average debt per creditor
1783/84	1.3296	20,282	17,622	35,010	15,254	13,254	2,000	26,331	1.73	49	714
1784/85	1.3726	20,826	18,951	**33,158**	15,162	13,759	1,403	**24,157**			
1785/86	1.4173	21,370	20,280	31,306	15,070	14,265	806	22,089		53	591
1786/77	1.4630	21,914	21,609	32,055	14,979	14,770	209	21,910	1.46	58	553
1787/88	1.5104	25,113	24,571	**32,720**	16,627	16,268	359	**21,663**			
1788/89	1.5588	26,171	23,816	33,384	16,789	15,278	1,511	21,416	1.28	63	530
1789/90	1.6089	27,262	23,941	34,384	16,944	14,880	2,064	21,371	1.26	62	555
1790/91	1.6610	28,359	25,924	34,688	17,073	15,608	1,466	20,884	1.39	57	609
1791/92	1.7151	28,139	23,623	34,736	16,406	13,773	2,633	20,253	1.22	57	609
1792/93	1.7700	30,779	25,368	32,316	17,389	14,332	3,057	18,258	1.09	52	621
1793/94	1.8271	34,644	29,328	32,594	18,961	16,052	2,909	17,839	0.94	52	627
1794/95	1.8860	32,121	28,350	32,354	17,031	15,032	1,999	17,155	1.01	55	588
1795/96	1.9474	29,578	24,965	30,495	15,188	12,820	2,369	15,659	1.03	48	635
1796/97	2.0102	30,825	26,809	29,445	15,334	13,336	1,998	14,648	0.96	46	640
1797/98	2.0745	29,938	25,115	29,940	14,432	12,107	2,325	14,432	1.00	49	611
1798/99	2.1420	31,264	34,602	35,600	14,596	16,154	-1,558	16,620	0.88	56	636
1799/1800	2.2115	36,160	35,016	42,021	16,351	15,834	517	19,001	1.12	63	667
1800/01	2.2824	39,494	39,729	43,266	17,304	17,407	-103	18,956	1.25	64	676
1801/02	2.3564	37,811	31,750	40,143	16,046	13,474	2,572	17,036	1.11	66	608
1802/03	2.4328	33,655	35,044	42,918	13,834	14,405	-571	17,642	1.22	61	704
1803/04	2.5116	35,727	30,657	41,508	14,225	12,206	2,019	16,527	0.87	57	728
1804/05	2.5927	37,308	31,152	41,408	14,390	12,015	2,375	15,971	0.94	57	726
1805/06	2.6772	41,557	35,822	41,617	15,523	13,380	2,142	15,545	1.02	51	816
1806/07	2.7640	54,235	51,942	40,745	19,622	18,792	830	14,741	0.96	54	755
1807/08	2.8536	40,494	38,802	43,990	14,191	13,597	593	15,415	1.07	60	733
1808/09	2.9456	54,125	54,312	45,000	18,375	18,438	-64	15,277	0.81	62	726
1809/10	3.0412	55,974	56,290	57,016	18,405	18,509	-104	18,748	1.10	83	687
1810/11	3.1395	74,617	73,139	56,464	23,767	23,297	471	17,985	1.18	82	689
1811/12	3.2415	74,392	71,367	64,896	22,950	22,017	933	20,020	1.31	79	821
1812/13	3.3471	81,966	81,211	66,849	24,489	24,263	226	19,972	1.38	79	846
1813/14	3.4556	70,061	66,615	71,174	20,275	19,277	997	20,597	1.09	83	858
1814/15	3.5679	68,343	66,127	78,039	19,155	18,534	621	21,872	1.28	90	867
1815/16	3.6832	67,182	64,293	81,906	18,240	17,456	784	22,238	1.46	94	871
1816/17	3.8033	67,239	63,119	81,694	17,679	16,596	1,083	21,480	1.40	95	860
1817/18	3.9266	62,904	60,462	81,334	16,020	15,398	622	20,713	1.44	94	865
1818/19	4.0539	67,385	63,810	86,700	16,622	15,740	882	21,387	1.13	105	826
1819/20	4.1855	68,474	64,939	91,828	16,360	15,515	845	21,939	1.29	107	858
1820/21	4.3220	73,708	63,624	91,132	17,054	14,721	2,333	21,086	1.39	105	868

Balancing the accounts and facing unexpected destabilizing expenses: the importance of the "internal" credit market

The study of the annual balance sheets (see tables 3 and 4) shows that regular communal revenues (i.e. loans of any kind are not included) fully covered the regular and predictable expenses and usually left an annual profit. As a consequence, the accumulated debt was partly amortized and the "external" and high-interest-bearing bonds were substituted with "internal" and low-interest bonds.[84] This was reversed in years of war and internal turmoil, when the Ottoman central and provincial authorities imposed heavy extraordinary levies (among them the *sürsat, iştira, zahire baha*, and *imdad-ı seferiye*). Total expenses soared in both nominal and real terms. In this case money was sought from those that possessed it: usually from rich merchants, notables, and corporate bodies (charitable endowments, parish and monastic funds) of the community.

The community faced two serious moments of continually rising expenses. The first one was linked to the war in Egypt (1798–1803). Extraordinary levies mounted and the treasurer had to contract large loans and close his balances with a small loss (years 1799, 1801, 1803). Nevertheless, aided by the fact that the rapid devaluation of silver *guruş* contracted the *real* burden of ordinary lump-sum taxes, the communal finances once again rapidly stabilized. The second case of an unexpected rise in expenses erupted in the war years of 1806–12 and was a combination of two different processes: 1) extraordinary levies had once again risen and 2) new ordinary taxes (*iştira* and *bedel-i harir*) were imposed, while others had their lump sum raised. This kind of rapid rise in expenses was more threatening since the new governor of Thessaly (*sancak* of Tirhala), Velyuddin Paşa, farmed or was assigned the possession (*deruhde*) of most of the ordinary taxes. The dynasty of Ali Paşa Tepeleden and his sons Muhtar Paşa and Velyuddin Paşa was famous for its relentless accumulation of expropriated communities as *çiftlik* estates in Thessaly, Epirus, and continental Greece. This was secured with the use of aggressive military pressure by marauding bands of irregulars, heavy taxation and extortion of levies, combined with the (almost obligatory) offer by these magnates and their retinue of high-interest loans to the indebted "target" communes. Thanks to its notables, merchants, and prosperous artisans who were able to rapidly lend the necessary sum of money to the commune, Zagora did not suffer the same fate.

Of course, communal financial flexibility had its cost: the high percentage of the item of debt service in the annual account balance. This was not threatening by itself, but it could become, in its turn, a cause of financial destabilization (by increasing the annual communal expenses), a source of intracommunal factionalism and strife, and subsequently a stimulus of social unrest. Consequently, managing the internal communal debt was of primary importance. In Zagora, where capital was disposable even among modest households, this was obtained through careful management of the internal credit market and through a policy of substitution of higher- for lower-interest credit. There existed different money markets for different "investors." The creditors of the "external" debt expected the usual high interest of the regional market (15% for the Ottomans and 20% for the Jewish bankers) and consequently were rarely sought after and rapidly disbursed. The "internal" market grew flexible enough to provide more than one kind of credit. Some creditors expected relatively high interest (10%) and were ready to lend a substantial amount of money. They were usually the merchants and notables who had been instrumental in amortizing the large debt of the community in the third quarter of the eighteenth century. They tended to withdraw from the market once the community's need for money fell. Poorer members of the community invested in the communal debt bonds for longer periods of time (at 8%). Their aim was to secure a modest annual rent. Orphans and widows were common among them. The same is true for most of the loans lent by parish and monastic funds and special charitable endowments, which lent to the community considerable sums of money (at 6%).[85] From the beginning of the nineteenth century, a large part of the communal debt had become a long-term low-interest (6–8%) investment of rent-seeking members and institutional funds. These kinds of creditors offered low interest and long-term (or even perpetual in the case of endowments) credit, but were unable to respond quickly to the demand for large sums of money.

As a consequence, during the difficult years of rapidly rising expenses (1806/07–1812/13), a second "internal" money market was created and offered substantial amounts of short-term credit at a relatively high interest rate (1% monthly). Merchants and notables were once again those who offered the necessary money. This was not done for economic reasons, since they could have easily obtained higher interest rates for their disposable cash elsewhere. Nevertheless, it was of fundamental importance for them to preserve the communal *status quo* against Velyuddin Paşa. They offered their cash on short notice (for relatively modest interest) to make sure that the community would never be indebted to outsiders; then, once the pressure was off, they withdrew their capital and replaced it with low-interest-rate credit, coming from rent-seeking poorer members of the community or from various ecclesiastical and charitable funds (usually managed by these same notables).

Supporting Evidence from Other Communes in Epirus, Morea, and the Archipelago

The commune of Zagora was not exceptional. One can find other examples of communal finances with the same structure, that is with separate internal and external echelons, and with powerful and rich *kocabaşıs*, who were able on short notice to readily advance money to their community's treasurer and help him meet all kinds of unpredictable expenses.

A first good example is Trikkeri, an isolated small town on the southern edge of Pelion. It was a commune of sailors and ship owners,[86] and was attached to the Para-Naxa Mukataası possessed by the Ottoman Kapudan Paşa (see table 5).[87] In 1817/18 the commune treasurer paid 25,132 *guruş* of expenses and presented a balance loss of 4,028 *guruş* (16%). An amount of 2,878 *guruş* was borrowed to cover expenses. The head tax does not figure among either revenues or expenses. The largest items of the latter were the salaries and other expenses for the local sailors (*melah*) serving in the imperial fleet.[88] Other important taxes were the *mal-i iltizam* and the sheep tax (*celep*). The major source of revenues, totally unrelated to the expenses, consisted of contributions paid by each family according to an assessment register. Other revenue sources were the customs tax (*gümrük*) and some minor tithes. Expenses before debt service and arrears were equal to 20,871 *guruş*, while revenues (if arrears were normally paid) would be 21,468 *guruş* and cover the regular expenses. All creditors bear Christian names and some of them belong to known local families. It is clear that the commune was balancing its accounts through a flexible use of the internal credit market.

The major concurring example is that of Hydra, an island community that was the most prominent shipping center in the Archipelago in the half century before the Greek War of Independence. Hydra's loyalty to the Sublime Porte during the late-eighteenth-century wars against the Russians earned her

Table 4. The annual balance sheets of Zagora in constant *guruş*
(my own estimates in bold characters)

	(1)	(2)	(3)	(4)	(5)	Revenues	(6)	(7)	(8)	(9)	(10)	(11)	Expenses
1783/84	13,749	1,102		403		15,254	5,221		1,901	2,497	3,635	2,000	15,254
1784/85	**13,134**	**1,759**		**269**		15,162	**6,109**	**380**	**1,614**	**2,128**	**3,528**	**1,403**	15,162
1785/86	**12,520**	**2,416**		**134**		15,070	**6,998**	**761**	**1,326**	**1,758**	**3,422**	**806**	15,070
1786/77	11,905	3,074				14,979	7,886	1,141	1,039	1,388	3,315	209	14,979
1787/88	11,587	2,785	2,158	98		16,627	8,743	511	3,739	868	2,407	359	16,627
1788/89	12,738	3,057	647	348		16,789	**7,723**	**1,007**	**2,351**	**1,679**	**2,518**	1,534	16,813
1789/90	12,706	2,752		1,486		16,944	7,760	445	1,496	2,782	2,397	2,064	16,944
1790/91	11,357	2,862	855	1,999		17,073	6,932	1,495	3,199	1,651	2,331	1,466	17,073
1791/92	11,917	2,893	177	1,420		16,406	6,942	1,135	2,682	686	2,328	2,633	16,406
1792/93	11,567	2,961	310	2,552		17,389	7,690	1,742	2,202	658	2,039	3,057	17,389
1793/94	11,117	4,226	657	2,961		18,961	7,285	1,268	1,469	1,012	5,018	2,909	18,961
1794/95	13,571	2,772	433	255		17,031	7,785	755	1,062	3,332	2,098	1,999	17,031
1795/96	12,245	2,497	302	144		15,188	7,196	1,405	482	1,715	2,022	2,372	15,191
1796/97	11,320	2,885	298	830		15,334	7,048	863	746	1,845	2,834	1,997	15,334
1797/98	10,767	2,443	193	1,028		14,432	6,465	818		1,622	3,202	2,325	14,432
1798/99	10,146	2,718	446	1,286	1,559	16,155	6,979	1,084	4,756	2,179	1,156		16,154
1799/1800	10,648	2,936	2,767			16,351	6,902	963	4,519	910	2,541	519	16,353
1800/01	10,517	3,270	3,015	503	103	17,407	6,349	588	6,293	2,862	1,314		17,407
1801/02	10,144	3,287	2,615			16,046	6,658	1,137	1,446	2,011	2,222	2,571	16,045
1802/03	10,133	2,853	189	658	571	14,405	5,764	2,515	1,715	1,370	3,041		14,405
1803/04	10,203	2,742	1,280			14,225	5,710	1,607	797	2,063	2,029	2,019	14,225
1804/05	10,819	3,069	177	324		14,390	5,912	1,399	445	2,230	2,029	2,375	14,390
1805/06	11,602	3,026	564	330		15,523	6,199	1,473	2,190	2,213	1,306	2,142	15,523
1806/07	11,710	3,735	1,355	2,822	1,051	20,673	6,683	1,540	6,555	2,304	1,711	1,881	20,673
1807/08	9,848	3,115	403	824	794	14,985	5,716	1,272	1,132	1,386	4,091	1,387	14,985
1808/09	9,612	3,630	4,474	658	511	18,886	7,383	3,721	3,178	1,963	2,192	448	18,886
1809/10	10,375	3,624	4,125	282	702	19,107	7,620	2,275	2,286	1,269	5,059	598	19,107
1810/11	10,944	4,491	8,055	277	736	24,503	12,097	2,133	1,727	1,037	6,301	1,206	24,503
1811/12	13,058	4,312	5,105	476	550	23,500	9,929	1,733	2,212	1,690	6,452	1,483	23,500
1812/13	12,429	4,372	6,684	1,004	255	24,744	10,273	3,030	2,431	885	7,645	490	24,754
1813/14	11,529	3,663	4,590	492		20,274	8,697	2,393	309	1,757	6,121	997	20,274
1814/15	10,581	3,243	4,385	946	270	19,425	8,746	2,165	200	1,611	5,811	891	19,424
1815/16	10,144	3,474	3,807	815		18,240	8,770	1,540	630	1,617	4,899	784	18,240
1816/17	11,359	3,166	2,457	697		17,679	8,902	1,507	456	2,047	3,684	1,083	17,679
1817/18	11,105	2,615	1,710	589	79	16,098	8,770	1,217	381	1,852	3,178	701	16,099
1818/19	11,125	2,837	1,981	679		16,622	6,678	2,422	753	2,147	3,741	882	16,623
1819/20	10,585	3,050	1,871	854		16,360	7,352	1,138	1,950	1,649	3,426	845	16,360
1820/21	10,851	3,149	2,236	818	1,014	18,068	5,818	1,227	4,179	1,704	1,793	3,348	18,069
1783-1790	79.7%	15.3%	2.5%	2.5%		100 %	45.5%	3.8%	12.2%	11.8%	19.1%	7.6%	100 %
1791-1807	68.5%	18.5%	5.6%	6.2%	1.19%	100 %	41.3%	7.9%	14.6%	11.1%	14.2%	10.9%	100 %
1808-1821	57.2%	18.2%	19.3%	3.5%	1.8%	100 %	43.5%	10.3%	8.1%	8.4%	24.0%	5.6%	100 %

(1) "Internal" agricultural taxation and tithes (2) Windfalls, *cizye*, etc. (3) Newly contracted debt
(4) Transfers (5) Loss (6) Ordinary Taxes (7) Usual levies and *pişkeş* (8) Extraordinary levies
(9) Communal Expenses (10) Debt service and amortization (11) Profit

extensive fiscal privileges, as a sign of imperial satisfaction. Since that time, its ship-owners had built the largest merchant fleet in the Archipelago and they profited greatly, later, when prices of exports skyrocketed from the British blockade of continental Europe. A rich class of captains, merchants, and financiers emerged, which completely dominated the political and economic life of the island and took over the role of community representatives.

Table 5. Expenses and revenues in Trikkeri, January 1, 1817–November 4, 1818

Expenses	guruş	%	Revenues	guruş	%	%
mal-i iltizam	3,662	14.57%	Contributions by households	13,165	62.38%	52.38%
Expenses of sailors (melah)	7,323	29.14%	Customs and tithes	3,469	16.44%	13.80%
Tax on sheep (celep)	3,533	14.06%	Various undefined revenues	1,592	7.55%	6.34%
Undefined expenses and gifts	6,353	25.28%	Additional internal debt	2,878	13.64%	11.45%
Interest paid	1,020	4.06%	Sum of Revenues	21,104	100.00%	83.97%
Arrears	3,241	12.90%				
Sum of Expenses	25,132	100.00%	Loss	4,028	16.03%	16.03%

Hydra, an agriculturally destitute rocky small island, was one of the possessions of the Kapudan Paşa, and its main fiscal obligations (except for the *cizye*) were to send, twice a year, a specific number of sailors for the Imperial fleet and, in case of naval campaigns, to provide ships for duty as auxiliary vessels. Other taxes paid to Ottoman fiscal authorities were relatively insignificant.[89] As in Zagora, the head tithe (*cizye*) was directly assessed and collected by the communal officials and the aggregate sum was delivered to the *cizyedar*.[90] The largest single item of the yearly expenses was the one devoted to the salaries of the sailors and to all kind of extraordinary war levies. In order to pay for these taxes and for the additional local expenses (e.g. the salary of the local Christian militiamen—*kolcu*s) the community of Hydra produced its own *internal* revenue system. Its major revenue sources were the customs tax (*gümrük*) and a host of ordinary contributions paid by ship-owners[91] and shopkeepers,[92] as well as levies on sailors and other inhabitants, who were not members of the community. When expenses were rising and a large communal debt was contracted, there was an effort to amortize this debt or pay for the extraordinary expenses. A special tax (*tansa*)[93] was distributed among Hydriot households according to a register of assessment. This special tax was levied in 1802–1805 and for a last time in 1810. Other substantial communal expenses were the "charities made in the secretaries' lists" (*kala ginomena ton pagkon*), by which one must understand that accumulated arrears were written off. In order to balance the accounts, the chief treasurer and secretary (*katzilieris, cancelliere*) used to advance money to the communal treasury.

The balance accounts of Hydra for the years 1803–22 are not as neat and sophisticated as those of Zagora. There are small gaps in the documentation, a separate list of creditors was not maintained (or found), while profits and losses were not always reported in the relevant items of the accounts of the year to come. The communal officers were sometimes dismissed before the term of their office and each treasurer adopted his own method of itemizing revenues and expenses. Balance sheets were usually prepared each month (or trimester in 1812–15) and an aggregated balance sheet was produced every 10–14 months by the outgoing treasurer. We can thus have a relatively accurate view of every month's expenses and revenues. Every year expenses were concentrated in two or three months (see figure 2). Sometimes monthly (unexpected) expenses greatly exceeded the respective revenues. To pay them in time the treasurer had to borrow money from other rich members of the community. It is interesting to see that, for the whole period 1803–21, newly contracted debt made up almost 45% of the year's expenses (current profit and loss excluded). In the first half-period (Jan. 1803–Feb. 1812), the most important item of expenses was the one related to the contribution to the manning of the imperial fleet (35% on average). The collected *cizye* was

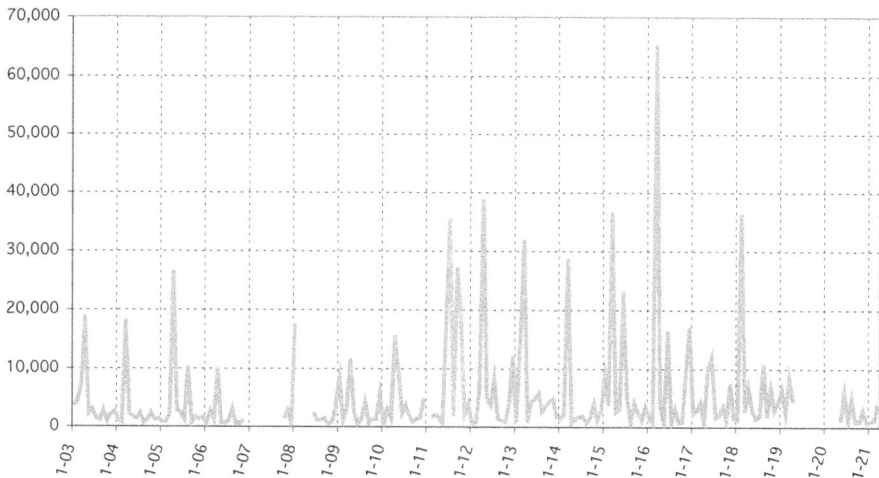

Figure 2. Hydra: the monthly expenses expressed in constant guruş (Jan. 1803–Mar. 1821)

Table 6. The mean annual revenues and expenses of Hydra
(as percentage of expenditure)[94]

REVENUE	1803–1811	1812–1819	1803–1819
tax (*tansa*) allotted to the households	13.61		10.23
cizye	3.49	1.12	1.96
gümrük	18.21	16.43	17.06
levies on ships	28.59	7.61	15.03
levies on foreigners and shopkeepers	3.76	6.97	6.61
various other revenues	3.46	0.47	2.36
irregular transfers	0.41	1.18	3.21
Revenue (w/o debt)	**71.53**	**33.78**	**46.80**
newly contracted debt	55.24	85.09	90.50
Revenue	**126.77**	**118.87**	**121.32**
EXPENDITURE	1803–1811	1812–1819	1803–1819
taxes and regular expenses	27.08		47.43
communal expenses	7.95		10.12
expenses of sailors	35.16		26.44
other expenses	3.59		10.79
writing off accumulated arrears (*kala ginomena*)	24.13		20.73
debt service	2.10		3.15
Expenditure	100.00	100.00	100.00
Profit	26.77	18.87	21.32

only 4% of expenses. The major sources of revenue were the levy on ships (29%), the customs tax (18%), and the *tansa* tax (13%). Revenues covered 71.5% of the expenses and the rest was covered through short- and medium-term loans. Overall, the communal accounts were balanced with a net profit (27%), which was used to write off arrears (24%) and to service the debt.

For the subsequent half-period (March 1812–March 1821) we do not have any itemized information on expenses. What we can observe is that the *internal* debt in the revenues soared to cover 67% of expenses, probably because the *tansa* assessment was discontinued and the levies on ships were substantially lowered. Only the customs tax revenue covered a substantial amount of expenses. In spite of this rise in debt servicing, the accounts were always balanced with a profit. But the real monthly average of expenses (expressed in terms of the constant *guruş* of 1775) rose by 60% from 3,425 in 1802–1812 to 5,482 constant *guruş* in 1812–1821. Revenues rose by only 40% and, as a consequence, the balance profit diminished by 17%. A flexible "internal" money market was thus essential in this case as well for the faultless communal financial performance, in spite of the frequent changes of treasurer.

There are of course cases where the administration of local finances took different forms. One such example is the villages of the Zagorya *nahiyesi*.[95] In these villages there was not a clear separation of the internal and the external echelons: every tax was distributed among the village households according to the local assessment register. Arrears and the various local expenses were inscribed in a separate account (the *bakiye* register) and were collected by the communal authorities. The *kocabaşı*s were no less powerful than in the above-examined cases of Pelion and the Archipelago. As we shall see later, they had been able to secure the assistance of Albanian *subaşı*, who enforced the collection of taxes and arrears. In poorer communities, as in the island of Skyros in 1817,[96] which had no powerful and influential *kocabaşı*s,

Table 7. The annual balance sheets of Hydra
(my own estimates for monthly revenue and expenditure)

Period Day/mo./yr.	Revenue			Expenditure in *guruş*	loss or profit in *guruş*	%	no of months	Monthly in constant *guruş*		
	guruş w/debt	*guruş* w/o debt	% debt					year	Expend.	Revenue w/o debt
1/3/1795–1/3/1796	28,984	28,361	2%	28,984			12	1795	1,240	1,213
1803	141,379	141,379		122,293	19,086	16%	12	1803	4,189	4,843
1804	121,287	102,817	21%	86,409	34,878	40%	12	1804	2,867	3,411
1805	201,123	130,188	53%	134,433	66,690	50%	12	1805	4,321	4,184
1/1 to 30/12/1806	82,862	59,685	40%	58,037	24,826	43%	11	1806	2,150	2,211
1/10/1807–31/1/1808 and 1/6–31/12/1808	136,544	35,432	108%	93,272	43,272	46%	11	1808	3,347	1,271
1809	167,307	118,986	40%	121,715	45,592	37%	12	1809	3,443	3,366
1810	159,383	118,731	29%	140,049	19,334	14%	12	1810	3,838	3,130
1/2/1811–1/3/1812	402,466	89,719	87%	357,929	44,537	12%	13	1811	8,770	2,198
1/3/1812–1/3/1813	348,868	80,262	85%	314,737	34,131	11%	12	1812	8,091	2,063
1/3/1813–1/3/1814	239,441	58,306	80%	227,161	12,280	5%	12	1813	5,656	1,452
1/3/1814–1/3/1815	220,780	46,453	88%	197,545	23,235	12%	12	1814	4,764	1,120
1/3/1815–1/3/1816	311,662	50,738	87%	299,683	11,979	4%	12	1815	7,000	1,185
1/3/1816–1/3/1817	473,409	64,342	194%	211,149	262,260	124%	12	1816	4,777	1,456
1/3/1817–1/5/1818	355,241	60,028	85%	349,148	6,093	2%	14	1817	6,557	1,127
1/5/1818–1/5/1819	215,495	73,505	67%	212,045	3,450	2%	12	1818	4,500	1,490
1/5/1819–1/5/1820	131,565	131,565		122,292	9,272	8%	12	1819	2,514	2,498
1/5/1820–1/4/1821	111,313	111,313		100,832	10,481	10%	11	1820	2,190	2,418

the village headmen simply assessed the fiscal capacity of each household and provided a written list to the Ottoman tax-farmers, who actually collected the tax due. In this case, the temptation of the Ottoman tax collector to personally benefit from his position was much greater.

Larger Examples: The Management of District Finances

Up to now we have examined the structure of communal finances in the context of a single Christian territorial community, like Zagora and Hydra. In some cases, as in the eighteenth–century Ottoman Morea, local self-government was *officially* extended to both the *kaza* and the *vilayet* echelons. Every territorial community sent its representatives to the *kaza* council, where important decisions were made concerning the assessment and collection of taxes and the local security and administration in general. The notables of each *kaza* sent their representative to the *vilayet* in order to form a provincial council, which assisted the *vali*'s *divan* in its administrative and fiscal functions.[97] It should be underlined that at the *kaza* level a large number of communities of diverse ethnic and confessional composition or of different economic profile were cooperating under the guidance of the *kadı* and the most prominent local *ayan* and *kocabaşı*s. Usually a *kaza* or a *nahiye* formed a single fiscal unit (*mukataa*) and was administered by a *voyvoda*.[98] All the above-mentioned officers were thus involved in local power networks. Our sole quantitative Greek case is that of the Karytaina *kazası* in Morea for the financial year 1819/20.[99]

In the Karytaina *kazası*, as well, two characteristics of paramount importance clearly stand out: 1) most taxes[100] and levies paid (as shown in the expenses) to the Ottoman overlords had no relation to the contributions collected from every one of the 106 communities comprising the *kaza*; 2) a large part of annual expenses were covered by short-term loans. As a result, total expenses of 604,178 *guruş* were paid to the various Ottoman authorities and creditors. Revenues were collected from each community according to a predefined matrix, i.e. the total sum of expenses was distributed among the 106 village and small-town communities and each community paid its due. That year 8.6% of expected total contributions of 423,085 *guruş* was in arrears. Arrears and urgent expenses were covered with loans that were disbursed the next year. In 1819/20, new loans of 217,364 *guruş* were contracted: 123,548 *guruş* (57% of the total sum) from Muslims and the rest from Christians, both individuals (36%) and communes (7%). The disbursed debt of the previous year 1818/19 amounted to 181,136 *guruş*. Most of it (101,777 *guruş*) was again owed to Muslims and the rest to Christians (individuals 35%, communes 9%).

It is interesting that the proportion of Christian and Muslim creditors does not change: 56–57% for the Muslims and 43–44% for the Christians. The same is true of the important individual creditors: among Muslims the *voyvoda* Mustafa Ağa dominated with 37.5% of the disbursed debt and 40% of the new loans, followed by the *bina emini* Hacı Yusuf Ağa (5.5% and 3.5% respectively). Among Christians, three families (Gheorghiou, Tambakopoulos, and Papayiannopoulos) offered 27% of the disbursed debt and 16% of the new loans. The interest (20% yearly) was high and the debt service amounted to 212,797 *guruş*, or 35% of total expenses! The newly contracted loans (217,364 *guruş*) covered 36% of total revenues. Year after year, the same people advanced high-interest money to the *kaza* to pay for its expenses, cover its arrears, and service its debt.

In this *kaza*, as much as in the above-examined communes, the rise of local self-government created a fiscal administration with comparable basic elements which comprise 1) a twin financial system with the taxes paid to the various overlords being unrelated to the contributions collected by individuals or communes; 2) a local credit market, which gave flexibility to the functioning of the system; and, finally, 3) a small group of notables, Muslim and Christians, who financially and socially predominated. But in this case—and this is the important difference from the previously examined examples—it seems that the *voyvoda* was the most powerful local agent, clearly surpassing in economic power and social prestige the Muslim *ayan* and the Christian *kocabaşı*.

A different structure is that of the exclusively Christian Zagorya *nahiyesi*, dominated by its powerful *kocabaşı*, among whom one was selected as their collective representative: the *başkocabaşı* of the *nahiye*. Consequently the power of alternative power centers, like the *kadı* or the bishop, was relatively restrained.[101] Zagorya notables extensively lent money to the communities and to their townsfolk. They also sub-farmed local taxes and collaborated with the provincial *ayan*.[102] They were fully in charge of the fiscal assessment and collection, as well as of the maintenance of public security, and they had minor forensic powers. The *kocabaşı* were powerful enough to command total communal compliance to their will and rich enough to provide the necessary credit to the communities and the individual peasants. It seems that they cooperated smoothly with the provincial magnates who governed from Ioannina, like Ali Paşa Tepeleden, and they were usually sub-farmers of various local taxes, like the sheep tax (*celep*) and the customs tax. Zagorya communities were rarely transformed into *çiftliks*,[103] in spite of the turbulent area in which they were situated.

On some occasions the *kocabaşıs* were co-operating with the Albanian *subaşıs* (meaning locally both a usurer and a steward or power-enforcer) in order to impose their rule and secure the collection of arrears, through the so-called *ağalik* contract. In 1828, for instance, an Albanian *subaşı*, Cenel Ağa, was employed by the commune of *Tsepelovo* for a year as a law-enforcer, a treasurer, and a tax and arrears collector: "as a *subaşı* and a *deruhde* of our community." He was supposed to collect the arrears and the other tax contributions according to lists given to him by the *kocabaşı*. He serviced the commune's debt and forced payment of the money owed to the commune. He also advanced money—up to a certain amount—to pay for unexpected extraordinary levies and other expenses (*nüzül, harc-ı vilayet, kaftan-bahası*, etc.). He would receive an annual salary of 1,000 *guruş*, have his expenses covered, and gain an *ad valorem* profit of 1% for every money collection. Cenel Ağa did not personally reside in Tsepelovo. It was his men who actually enforced the will of the *kocabaşı* and protected the community from marauders.[104] What is interesting is that the relation between the Ağa and the communes seemed to work to the profit of both parties. There is no record of a *subaşı* trying to profit from *ağalik* contracts and usurp peasant lands. It is clear that this type of contract secured the dominant position of the local notables and the independence of the small-owner community.

Competition over the Distribution of Fiscal Surplus

The next most important question which may be answered—with some precision—by our quantitative data is that of the distribution of the "fiscalized" surplus among the various contenders. By surplus I mean the part of the production that is not used to replace the consumed factors of production. In the Ottoman economy a large part of this surplus was captured in the form of taxes and other fiscal levies. We do not know the magnitudes involved in the local production of goods and services, but we can nevertheless try to study the distribution of the "fiscalized" surplus among those with a right to it: the treasury and the central state elite, the provincial magnates and *ayan*, and the Christian *kocabaşıs*.

Competition for the Fiscal Surplus among the Ottoman Elite

The reign of Selim III was a turning point in Ottoman politics. Recent studies have pointed to the fact that a growing number of members of the central state elite had reached the conclusion—after the catastrophic experience of the wars against the Habsburg Emperor and the Czar in the second half of the eighteenth century—that the politics of "provincialization" were wearing out the financial and hence the military force of the empire.[105] Selim and his followers were engaged in a conscious effort to reclaim *malikâne* grants and other dilapidated fiscal sources, to impose new taxes, to discipline the provincial administration, and to finance and build a "new model" army. He was toppled, in spite of the fact that he had managed to secure the support of some of the provincial magnates and *ayan*. The first years of the reign of Mahmud II were once again a period of dominance by provincial magnates. Only gradually and carefully did Mahmud and his inner circle once again build an alliance that would prove strong enough to bring the provincial magnates under control and, finally, to destroy the power of the Janissaries and to engage the empire in sweeping reforms.

Using the data from Zagora we can have a precise view of the competition for surplus between the central state and the provincial magnates and *ayan* (see figure 3). Three main conclusions can be reached:

1. In the long run, the rise of taxes and levies could not match the high rates of currency devaluation and of silver depreciation relative to gold. This helped the communal leadership reduce the surplus captured by Ottoman authorities, and maintain, in the long run, in real and not in nominal terms, a steady global taxation (see figure 1).

2. In years of peace and low extraordinary taxation and hence of profits in the balance of accounts and of debt amortization, the percentage of total expenses that is "destined" for the central state elite (the

central treasury and the harem administration) in Istanbul is high.
The contrary is true for the war years of high taxation, when the
part of provincial magnates and *ayan* soared.

3. In general, of course, years of war were years of growing real taxation in absolute figures (see table 4). Yet, during the reign of Selim,
   in war years, the levies destined both for the central state elite and
   for the provincial magnates and *ayan* were growing. This changed
   during the first years of the reign of Mahmud. Then, it was mainly
   the provincial magnates that profited from war taxation. From 1808,
   the provincial magnate family of Velyuddin Paşa and his father Ali
   Paşa of Ioannina captured a large percentage of all expenses, reduc-
   ing the income sent to Istanbul. This was only reversed in fiscal
   year 1820/1821, when the Sublime Porte turned against this rebel
   provincial magnate family.

In other words, the rise of *ayan* and provincial magnates, related to their
capacity of capturing a larger part of the fiscal surplus, was facilitated in
years of war and internal anarchy. At the same time, in opposition to this

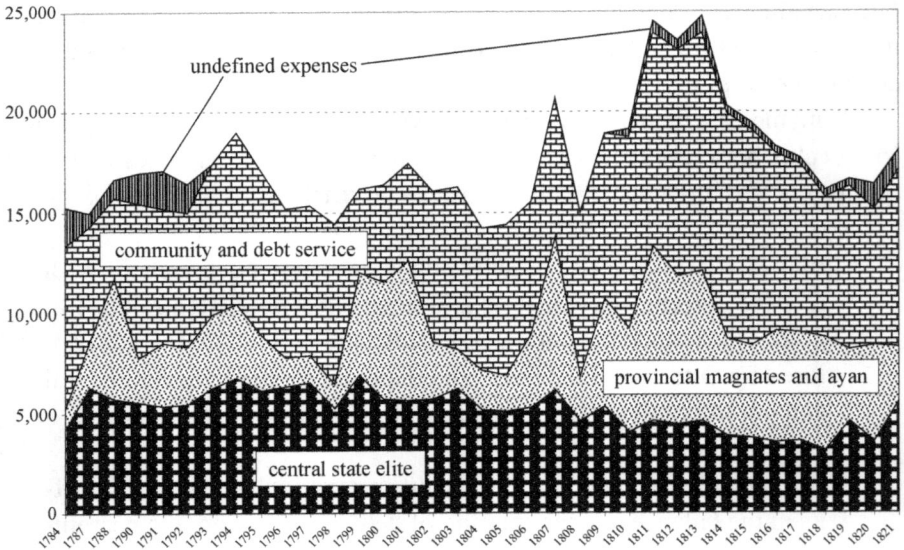

Figure 3. Distribution of expenses among various groups (in constant *guruş*)

increase in power of the ayan and provincial magnates, there occurred a convergence of interests between the central state and the taxpayers. But it must also be underlined that the growing power of the communal notables, in an age of demographic growth and galloping inflation, undercut the fiscal surplus accruing to the central state elite in favor of this Christian local elite. Thus the *kocabaşıs* captured, through their domination of the credit and commercial network, the growing surplus left to the producer. In effect, any part of the surplus that was not captured by the Ottoman overlord was to be either consumed *in situ* or devolved to the other mechanisms of surplus extraction (land rent, artisan, commercial, and financial profit).

The Portion of Expenses Spent Locally

In any commune, part of the expenses was not captured by the central state and the provincial elite but was spent locally. In the communities where the internal credit market was predominant, as in Pelion and Hydra, debt service was primarily a source of income for local rent-seekers. In Zagora the part destined for the central and provincial elite would fluctuate between 47% and

Table 8. Regular expenses of the community of Miliais (1806) [106]

Expenses	guruş	%
payment of *mukataa*	7,000	30.16%
kara astar and *celep*	430	1.85%
resm-i zacriye	1,100	4.74%
pişkeş to "our lords"	500	2.15%
Subtotal to the central state elite	**9,030**	**38.91%**
maktu payment (to Velestino)	1,200	5.17%
kapi parası (to Larissa)	350	1.51%
umur-i şeri (to the *kadı* of Leivadia)	80	0.34%
maktu payment (to the *voyvoda* of Argalast Mukataası, at Karabasi)	45	0.19%
amilik payment to the *zabid*	1,200	5.17%
Subtotal to the Ottoman provincial elite	**2,875**	**12.39%**
ulûfe of *derbentçi* militia	2,000	8.62%
levy of the Metropolitan bishop	50	0.22%
expenses for the rural guards	400	1.72%
paid to the communal secretary	200	0.86%
other regular expenses	1,500	6.46%
Subtotal to the *kocabaşı* and local militia	**4,150**	**17.88%**
regular interest payments	4,200	18.10%
interest payments of new loans	2,955	12.73%
Debt service subtotal	**7,155**	**30.83%**
Total sum	**23,210**	**100.00%**
Total sum (in constant *guruş*)	**8,670**	

79%, the average being 62.5%. In Miliais, this percentage fell to 50%, but the head tithe was not included (see table 8). If the *cizye* was included, the average percentage would probably be closer to that of Zagora. In Hydra, in 1803–1811, the average respective percentage is more difficult to calculate, but it was certainly less than 66% of total expenses. I think that, as a rule of thumb, we can say that the central and provincial elite captured on average less than two thirds of total communal expenses.

Fiscal Charge per Household: A Constant or a Slowly Growing Index?

It is interesting to note that this period of rapid "inflation" of prices measured in current silver *guruş* was not detrimental to the communal finances. Total taxation in real (gold) terms did not seem to change in Zagora (see table 3). Currency devaluation profited borrowers, farmers, and merchants at the expense of lenders, the state treasury, and rent-seekers. It profited the Zagora community at the expense of the treasury.

More interesting is the fact that all the information on per capita aggregate taxation taken from the balance accounts of communal finances seem to point to the same level of taxation: 14–34 constant *guruş* (or 3.5–8.5 Venetian gold pieces) per household (see table 9). This is quite a narrow margin, and of course differences can be ascribed to a possible error in the number of households. I believe that 20–24 *guruş* per household (5–6 gold pieces) can be considered more or less credible as an average taxation per household. In per capita this would be 4–6 *guruş* or 1–1.5 gold pieces, figures that are not very far from the equivalent ones of the French Ancien Régime.[107]

Of course some communes were more privileged than others. The maritime community of Hydra was the least imposed upon, thanks to its extensive privileges, the complete control over its finances by the central state elite (*kapudan paşa*), and the socioeconomically powerful class of local *kocabaşıs*. On the other hand we find the Karytaina *kazası*, which must be closer to the average position of rural districts, where Muslim and Christian notables dominated local politics and captured a large part of the produced surplus.

A second observation is that aggregate taxation increases (both in nominal and in real terms) after 1808, a period characterized by the complete domination of provincial magnates. This is at least what the only two series of quantitative data we possess (for Hydra and Zagora) indicate. This is probably true for taxation per household. It is further evidence that in the pre-

Tanzimat era one of the most important social factors was the implicit conflict over surplus between Muslim provincial magnates and *ayan* on the one hand and the Christian rural communities (and possibly all poorer peasants irrespective of religion) on the other. It is possible that this brought together the Christian peasants and the Imperial House more than we usually think.

The final victory of the central state elite over the rebellious provincial magnates and the disciplining of the provincial elite (*ayan* and *kocabaşıs*) helped the concentration of fiscal sources and revenues. The 1841 per household taxation of Pelion[108] in real terms (26 *guruş* per household) is higher than the rates observed in Zagora, Trikkeri, and Miliais before 1821. Does this indicate an increase in per capita taxation after the Greek War of Independence, the centralization of administrative power, and the 1839 fiscal reforms? I believe that this is a strong hypothesis.

Conclusion

The fiscal and administrative transformations of the eighteenth century engendered a new distribution of fiscal resources and power among the governing classes, i.e. the central state elite, the provincial magnates, and local notables (*ayan* and *kocabaşı*). This new equilibrium gave unprecedented autonomy in administrative and fiscal matters to the local elite, both Muslim and Christian. It also secured for them unsuspected sources of enrichment. The control of these fiscal and power resources emerged as the principal objective of these provincial elites. The bitter opposition of contending political factions in many local societies (Muslim and non-Muslim) was the immediate result of this process. These factions brought together local notables, provincial magnates, and other power brokers in the central state elite.

There was a growing cleavage between the Christian *kocabaşıs* and their Muslim counterparts, as there was an implicit convergence of interest, at least from the final decades of the eighteenth century, between the central government and the Christian communal notables. The *kocabaşıs* had little prospect of land accumulation and limited ambitions of political and social mobility. No matter how enriched by merchant and financial activities, they were bound to the protective shield of their territorial community, which was a source of economic gain, social prestige, and political power. Securing

Table 9. Estimation of the per household taxation in various Christian communities[109]

	Households	Guruş	Constant guruş	Constant guruş per household	Correction coefficient	Corrected per household
Zagora (1815)	800	69,045	19,352			24.19
Zagora (1784–1790)		24,598	16,457			20.57
Zagora (1791–1807)		35,263	16,294			20.37
Zagora (1808–1821)		67,330	19,163			23.95
Trikkeri (1817–1818)	310	25,132	6,401	20.65	1.39	28.74
Miliais (1806)	420	23,210	8,670	20.64	1.16	23.94
Miliais (1806–10)		32,116	11,254			26.80
Vakıflı villages of Argalast Mukatasi (taxes of *mal-i maktu, cizye, resm-i zacriye, mizan-i harir* in 1806)						
Makrinitza	892	18,964	7,084	7.94	2.15	17.07
Drakia	390	23,504	8,779	22.51	2.15	48.40
AgLavrentis	310	20,445	7,637	24.63	2.15	52.96
AgGiorgis	410	25,071	9,365	22.84	2.15	49.11
Vizitsa	122	6,962	2,601	21.32	2.15	45.83
Pinakates	122	8,657	3,234	26.50	2.15	56.98
Karabasi	48	2,897	1,082	22.54	2.15	48.47
Argalasti	798	33,192	12,398	15.54	2.15	33.40
Lafkos	510	16,693	6,235	12.23	2.15	26.29
Promyri	252	12,907	4,821	19.13	2.15	41.13
Mouressi	102	5,055	1,888	18.51	2.15	39.80
Kissos	252	6,157	2,300	9.13	2.15	19.62
Anilio	152	3,774	1,410	9.27	2.15	19.94
Makrirahi	102	2,955	1,104	10.82	2.15	23.27
Total *vakıflı* villages	4,462	187,233	69,936	15.67	2.15	33.70
Karytaina (1819/20)[a]	5,742	423,042	101,073	17.60	1.50	26.40
Karytaina (1819/20)[b]		604,178	144,350	25.14	1.50	37.71
Morea (1794)	80,000	3,000,000	1,642,000	20.52	1.15	23.60
Hydra mean[a]	4,889		27,699			5.67
Hydra mean[b]			68,201			13.95
Hydra (1803–1811)[a]			36,646			7.50
Hydra (1803–1811)[b]			63,009			12.89
Hydra (1812–1821)[a]			19,746			4.04
Hydra (1812–1821)[b]			72,816			14.89
Pelion (1841)	8,889	3,200,000	228,571	25.71	1.20	30.86

[a]expenses without debt amortization   [b]expenses with debt amortization

the administrative independence and the small-owner independence of their fellow townsfolk was the precondition for preserving their own power base. Their principal opponents were the Muslim notables and provincial magnates, who tried to transform independent peasant communities into *çiftlik*s.

In this effort their main means of defense was the firm administration of the communal finances, in order to secure the immediate payment of taxes, and the concentration of sufficient power of enforcement, in order to protect the community from marauders and to secure the compliance of its members with their decisions. Both means can be reduced to one: the mobilization of economic resources (Their own and others') in order to respond to any possible fiscal demand and to finance the necessary protective mechanisms. The prosperous Christian communities were those with the richest *kocabaşı* who could achieve the above-mentioned aim.

All the fiscal and financial communal structures examined above shared some common characteristics. Communal treasurers ensured that expected revenues (collected from every household according to an internal assessment system) were sufficient to amply cover regular expenses. A large local capital base would ensure that, in case of unexpected expenses, an *internal* credit market would provide low-interest loans in a timely fashion, without indebting the commune to outsiders, a permanent source of danger. This strategy secured the internal cohesion of the commune, allocated without bias the fiscal burden to all its members, and, minimizing over-taxation, secured for the dominant *kocabaşı* the possibility of extracting a larger part of the surplus that was left in the hands of the producer. The relative stability of the taxation per household in such communes shows that this was achieved, at least in the early nineteenth century.

Notes

1. The administrative and juridical district of a kadı.
2. Cf. R. A. Abu el-Haj, *Formation of the Modern State: the Ottoman Empire, 16th to 18th centuries* (Albany: SUNY Press, 1991); A. Salzmann, "An Ancien Régime Revisited: 'Privatization' and Political Economy in the 18th century Ottoman Empire," *Politics and Society* 21, no. 4 (1993): 393–423; L. Darling, *Revenue-Raising and Legitimacy: Tax Collection and Finance Administration in the Ottoman Empire, 1560–1660* (Leiden: E.J. Brill, 1996).
3. The view of the Ottoman Empire as a variant of the Asiatic Mode of Production model is a politically radical version of this same essentialist view, cf. H. Inan-Islamoglu, "Introduction: Oriental Despotism in World System Perspective," in H. Inan-Islamoglu, ed., *The Ottoman Empire and the World Economy* (Cambridge: Cambridge University Press, 1987), 1–24.
4. Ever since Byzantine times, territorial communities had been collectively held

responsible, by state authorities, for the payment of the assessed taxes; see H. Antoniadis-Bibicou and A. Guillou, "Problèmes d'histoire de la communauté villageoise byzantine et post-byzantine," in *Actes du Congrès franco-hellénique: Le monde rural dans l'aire méditerranéenne* (Athens: E.K.K.E.: K.N.E./ E.I.E, 1988), 47–48.

5. Even as late as 1813, in the printed Status (καταστατικόν) of the urban commune (*koinon*) of Melenikon which dealt in detail with the financial management of common property, with the financing and superintendance of schools and parish churches, and with the regulation of the cooperation between Christian communal officials, the church hierarchy, and parish officers, no reference whatsoever was made to the relationship of the Christian community with the Ottoman central and provincial administrative and fiscal authorities or with the non-Christian population of the city; see G. Kontogiorgis, Κοινωνική Δυναμική και Πολιτική Αυτοδιοίκηση. Οι Ελληνικές Κοινότητες της Τουρκοκρατίας (Athens: Ekdosis A. Livanes "Nea Synora", 1982), 425–38.

6. B.J. Slot [*Archipelagus Turbatus: Les Cyclades entre colonisation latine et occupation ottomane, c. 1500–1718* (Istanbul: Nederlands Historisch-Archaeologisch Instituut te Istanbul, 1982), 106–107, 176] has already underlined this fundamental difference between the respective Venetian and the Ottoman policies toward the communal institutions. The former was willing to fully integrate the communal representation in its provincial administrative system, which was organized according to a "territorially" represented social space. On the contrary, the Ottoman provincial administration represented the social space along confessional lines, according to the *millet* principle, and never formally integrated the communal representatives into its structure.

7. For details about the fiscal privileges of several groups of villages (providing special services and goods) in the plain of Thessaloniki in the seventeenth and eighteenth centuries, see V. Dimitriadis, "Φορολογικές κατηγορίες των χωριών της Θεσσαλονίκης κατά την Τουρκοκρατία," *Makedonika* 20 (1980): 413–31.

8. See A. Anastasopoulos, *Imperial Institutions and Local Communities: Ottoman Karaferye, 1758–1774*, Ph.D. dissertation (Cambridge, 1999), chapter 4. E. Gara, "In Search of Communities in 17th Century Ottoman Sources: The Case of the Karaferye District," *Turcica* 30 (1998): 143–44, has pointed out that by the 1740s the representation of village communities, which was occasionally noted in the archives starting in the early decades of the seventeenth century, was "institutionalized" in the *kaza* of Karaferye (Verroia) during the repartition of taxes. For seventeenth-century Muslim village communities of Western Anatolia, see H. Gerber, *The Social Origins of the Modern Middle East* (Boulder, Colo.: L. Rienner, 1987), 40–41.

9. The term *ayan* was unfortunately used indiscriminately to designate both the

Muslim notables who were locally distinguished by their economic power and social prestige, but who had no recognized status or official administrative function, and the powerful provincial magnates who were officially appointed as governors, etc. Hereafter, I will use the term *ayan* only for the class of local notables, from whom the (de jure or de facto) representatives of the local Muslim population were chosen. These local dynasties of notables have their exact parallel in the Christian *kocabaşı*. However, I will not differentiate between the *ayan* (and *kocabaşı*) who actually represented the local population and held an office like the *ayanlık* (and the *kocabaşılık*), and those who were, in general, members of notable families. Furthermore, hereafter I will restrict the use of the term "provincial magnates" for those powerful Muslim notables who had been appointed to official posts of governance (such as *paşa, mütesellim,* etc.). One should add at this point that the major difference between a Muslim *ayan* and a Christian *kocabaşı* was that the latter were disinclined to accumulate large portions of lands and other real estate and could not, of course, nurture hope for social advancement in the *rical* status. See above, p. 13.

10. Cf. Salzmann, "An Ancien Régime . . .," 404–405.

11. The official policy of clemency and accommodation to win over the newly conquered Christian territories.

12. Cf. E. Zachariadou, "Εφήμερες απόπειρες για αυτοδιοίκηση στις Ελληνικές πόλεις κατά τον ιδ' και ιε' αιώνες" *Ariadne* 5 (1989): 345–51.

13. Later, in the eighteenth and nineteenth centuries, the proprietor of large landholdings (*çiftlik sahibi*) and his representative (*subaşı*) assumed the same function.

14. See H. İnalcık and D. Quataert, eds., *An Economic and Social History of the Ottoman Empire, 1300-1914* (henceforth *ESHOE*) (Cambridge: Cambridge University Press, 1994), 134; J.C. Alexander, *Toward a History of Post-Byzantine Greece: The Ottoman Kanunnames for the Greek Lands, c. 1500–c. 1600* (Athens: J.C. Alexander, 1985), 193 and 370; and Slot, op. cit., 214–15, for the islands of the Archipelago in 1670.

15. See E. Grozdanova, "Les fondements économiques de la commune rural dans les régions bulgares (XVe–XVIIIe siècles)," *Études Balkaniques* 10/1 (1974): 32–34, and Anastasopoulos, loc. cit.

16. Even in *timar* villages, where the residing *sipahi*, or his representative, was supposed to ensure security and fully control all the possible sources of fiscal revenue, it was not unusual that the community rented out for its own profit the collectively held pastures and wastelands, even though the Ottoman law codes did not formally recognize communal collective property over *mevat* land; see S. Asdrachas, "Οι φορολογικές και περιοριστικές λειτουργίες των κοινοτήτων στην Τουρκοκρατία," in Ibid., Οικονομία και Νοοτροπίες (Athens: Hermes, 1988), 130; G. Papageorgiou, Οικονομικοί και κοινωνικοί

μηχανισμοί στον ορεινό χώρο: Ζαγόρι (μέσα 18ου–αρχές 20ού αιώνα) (Ioannina: Ekdosis Rizareiou Scholis, 1995), 60–61; and, for the Bulgarian lands, Grozdanova, op. cit., 37–39.

17. Cf. S. Petmezas, "L'organisation ecclésiastique sous la domination Ottomane," in P. Odorico, ed., *Conseils et Mémoires de Synadinos, prêtre de Serrès en Macédonie (XVIIe siècle)* (Paris/Athens: Editions de l'Association "Pierre Belon", 1996), 523–32.

18. Cf. Petmezas, "L'organisation ecclésiastique . . .," 503–506.

19. The "Chronicle of Synadinos, priest of Serres" of the first half of the seventeenth century is an invaluable source for the study of the (informal) urban communal organization, which was intimately related to the parish organization of the Church and the local guild system; see S. Petmezas, "La région et la ville de Serrès sous les Ottomans (XVe–XVIIIe siècles)," in P. Odorico, ed., *Conseils et Mémoires de Synadinos, prêtre de Serrès en Macédoine (XVIIe siècle)* (Paris/Athens: Editions de l'Association "Pierre Belon", 1996), 470–85.

20. Cf. Petmezas, "L'organisation ecclésiastique . . .," 518–32, and for a quantified estimation for the island of Myconos in 1620, see Slot, op. cit., 107 and 292–93.

21. Cf. P. Skoutzes, Απομνημονεύματα. Η τυραννία του Χατζή-Αλή Χασεκή στην Τουρκοκρατούμενη Αθήνα *(1772–1796)*, with an introduction by Th. Papadopoulos (Athens: Kedros, 1975), 138–39. The parish church had a courtyard with rooms, a kitchen, etc. Shelter and food were provided there for poor households and destitute older people. The parish officials coordinated all actions of social welfare and poor relief, including (compulsory) temporary employment as agricultural or industrial labor. In this way the communal leadership controlled the poor and alleviated social discontent. Parish councils involved in *cizye* collection on behalf of the *voyvoda* of Athens are evidenced as early as 1635–36; see Kontogiorgis, op. cit., 212–14. These communal activities of social welfare and poor-relief were formalized in the Charter of the Christian Community of Melnik (Meleniko), printed in Vienna in 1813; ibid., 431–32.

22. See Grozdanova, op. cit., 31, and *ESHOE*, 136.

23. See Petmezas, "L'organisation ecclésiastique . . .," 503–506.

24. Over-taxation was one of the main reasons for peasants fleeing. The decrease of the total number of households increased the per capita taxation and made the peasant economy more fragile. Peasant communities tried to prevent individual flight and, as a last resort, to organize the collective flight. Communal officers used the latter as a powerful argument in their negotiation of fiscal relief; cf. B. Hansen, "An economic model for Ottoman Egypt. The economics of collective tax responsibility," in A.L. Udovitch, ed., *The Islamic Middle East, 700–1900* (Princeton: Darwin Press, 1981), 476–77, and S. Asdrachas, "Le surplus rural

dans les régions de la Méditerranée orientale: les mécanismes," in *Économies Méditerranéennes. Équilibres et Intercommunications, XIIIe–XIXe siècles. Actes du IIe Colloque Internationale d'Histoire* (Athens: Centres de recherches néohelléniques, Foundation nationale de la recherche scientifique, 1986), ii: 43–45.

25. A large number of rules in customary family and civil law aimed to avoid the fragmentation of family farms or to promote their consolidation (pre-emption right or *protimisis*).

26. Secular and ecclesiastical authorities in the Christian communities strove by means of economic, social, or symbolic pressure to discourage their members from bringing a case to the *kadı* or to the Ottoman provincial authorities. Special attention was given to avoid any information on matters of criminal justice passing to the Ottoman official authorities.

27. See S. Asdrachas, "Οι φορολογικές και περιοριστικές . . ." 137–39; idem. "Νησιώτικες Κοινότητες: οι φορολογικές λειτουργίες" *Historica* 5 (1988): 256–57, and Papageorgiou, op. cit., 49–50.

28. Unfortunately, each scholar has different criteria for classifying taxpayers according to their assessed property and/or fiscal due, and these tables are not directly comparable. My own choice for Zagora was to use the Lorenz curve and the Gini coefficient of unequal distribution (1 as absolute inequality and 0 as absolute equality), which offer a standardized way to measure inequality; see S. Petmezas, *Recherches sur l'Économie et les Finances des villages du Pélion, région d'industries rurales, ca. 1750–1850*, Ph.D. dissertation (E.H.E.S.S., Paris, 1989), 573–4 and 581. My estimations of Zagora can be compared only with those of the island of Skyros (my own estimations using the data of M. Faltaits, Το τεφτέρι του κοινού Σκύρου του 1817 [Athens, 1973]) and of the 17 villages of the Koyuntepe *nahiyesi* as estimated by T. Güran, *Structure économique et sociale d'une région de campagne dans l'Empire ottoman vers le milieu du XIXe s. Étude comparée de neuf villages de la nahiye de Koyuntepe, Sanjak de Felib*e (Sofia: Centre international d'information sur les sources de l'histoire balkanique, 1979), 87.

29. In the eighteenth century, on the minuscule island of Serifos, with its poor agricultural economy, three families who paid 20–24% of the total taxation dominated the communal offices; see E. Liata, Η Σέριφος κατά την Τουρκοκρατία 17ος–18ος αιώνας (Athens: Hidryma Ereunas kai Paideias tis Emporikis Trapezas tis Hellados, 1987), 141–44.

30. Some early data are copies of Ottoman registers. This is the case for the islands of Mykonos (Slot, op. cit., 492–93), Andros, Milos, and Santorini (Balta and Spiliotopoulou, "Landed property and Taxation in Santorini in the 17th century," in E. Balta, *Problèmes et approches de l'Histoire ottomane* [Istanbul: Les Editions Isis, 1997], 122ff.). Later data are found in local registers, written by

communal secretaries and officers in Greek. This is the case for the islands of
Patmos (Asdrachas, "Νησιώτικες Κοινότητες . . .," 26–30), Serifos (Liata,
op. cit., 131–34), Skyros (Faltaits, op. cit.), and the proto-industrial township of
Zagora (Petmezas, *Recherches* . . ., chapters 9 and 10). Existing nineteenth-century registers from Miliais in Mount Pelion and Kepesovo (Papageorgiou, op.
cit., 74) in the mountainous Zagorya *nahiyesi*, near the city of Ioannina, have
not yet been studied in detail.

31. Cf. Balta and Spiliotopoulou, op. cit.

32. *Nahiye*: juridical sub-district; *sancak*: the basic military-administrative unit of
the Ottoman Empire; subdivision of a province.

33. Cf. Güran, loc. cit., and S. Draganova, "Différenciation de fortune dans les
villages de la Bulgarie du Nord-est durant les années 60–70 du XIXe siècle
(d'après des registres ottomans)," *Bulgarian Historical Review* 8, no. 2 (1980):
72. The Bulgarian cases seem more egalitarian than the Greek ones, because
of the minor role of non-agricultural income in the economies of the Bulgarian villages. If non-agricultural revenues were included in the Greek case, the
resulting outcome would certainly be less inegalitarian.

34. See H. İnalcık, "Fiscal and Military Transformation in the Ottoman Empire,
1600–1700," *Archivum Ottomanicum* 7 (1980): 311ff.

35. Public (*mirî*) lands whose tax revenues were formerly given to *sipahi* as *timar*
were recaptured by the Treasury and transformed into tax-units of land (*mukataalu*) whose revenue was leased out, see *ESHOE*, 108, 139–40. In general,
a large number of fiscal revenue sources that were previously distributed to
military, religious, and civil servants instead of a fixed salary to reward them
for their services, were reclaimed by the central government, packed into tax-
revenue units (*mukataa*), and leased out (*iltizam*) to tax-farmers (*multezim*) for
a short term (usually a three-year period) against direct cash instalments; see
ESHOE, 537–38. Through the *mukataa* system, the Ottoman treasury strove
to re-appropriate, regularize and monetize all yearly fiscal revenues. The term
mukataa is henceforward used only to describe "tax-revenue units" of any
kind. These units could be either directly managed by state officials (*emanet*) or
farmed out on a short-term basis (*iltizam*) or—after 1695—as life-long leases
(*malikâne*); see A. Tabakoğlu *Gerileme Dönemine Girerken Osmanlı Maliyesi*
(Istanbul: Dergâh Yayınları, 1985), 120–35.

36. See H. İnalcık, "Centralization and Decentralization in Ottoman Administration," in T. Naff and R. Owen, eds., *Studies in Eighteenth Century Islamic History* (Carbondale: Southern Illinois University Press, 1979), 31ff., and İnalcık,
"Fiscal and Military . . .," 335–37.

37. The voluminous information on seventeenth-century administrative and fiscal
functions of the Christian communities in the (usually small and poor) islands
of the Greek Archipelago is probably an exceptional phenomenon, related to

the permanent state of naval war between the Sublime Porte and Venice (Slot, op. cit.).

38. On the *malikâne* tax-lease, see *ESHOE*, 567–68, 713–15.

39. See Salzmann, "An Ancien Régime . . . ," especially 404–405. For a detailed analysis see A. Salzman, *Measures of Empire. Tax-farmers and the Ottoman Ancien Regime, 1695–1807* (Ph.D. dissertation, Columbia University, 1995), chapter 3.

40. *Maktuat* is just a form of tax assessment, i.e. the yearly payment by taxpayers of a pre-arranged lump sum irrespective of the real revenue of the taxed revenue source. As far as I can tell, one of the first references to a Greek community farming its own taxes is that of an unspecified island in the *sancak* of Naxos in the late sixteenth or early seventeenth century; cf. Darling, op. cit., 274.

41. Cf. Papageorgiou, op. cit., 74–75.

42. This, of course, from the point of view of the Ottoman treasury. Tax-farmers, provincial magnates, *ayan,* and *kocabaşı*s often had their own agendas, which openly opposed the interests of the local community and the Ottoman state.

43. See Petmezas, *Recherches . . . ,* 636–52, and Papageorgiou, op. cit., 44–47 and 156–58.

44. See İnalcık, "Fiscal and Military . . . ," 333–34.

45. Communities were collectively indebted, with their communal property (and sometimes the individual property of every member) as collateral (*malına kefil*). Of course the richer members (i.e. the notables) bore the greatest risk. It seems that this practice was discontinued in the Tanzimat era. In 1833, the community of Doliani in the Zagorya *nahiyesi*, later followed by others, formally abandoned the practice of collective responsibility for communal loans; see Papageorgiou, op. cit., 147–48.

46. In the city of Meleniko, in 1813, the communal charter provided that a 20-person electoral college, assisted by the local Bishop, would elect six communal officers, who then would in their turn select the parish councillors. Serving for at least one year was obligatory, and a penalty of 100 *guruş* (7.5 gold pieces) was imposed on those refusing their service! See Kontogiorgis, op. cit., 436.

47. See the early-nineteenth-century cases of Samos (A. Sevastakis, "Ποινική εξουσία των Μεγάλων Προεστών στην προεπαναστατική Σάμο," *Historica* 11 [1994]: 293–96), Miliais and Zagora (Petmezas, *Recherches . . . ,* 188–94).

48. See the late eighteenth century cases of Trikkala (I. Oikonomou, Ιστορική τοπογραφία ενός μέρους της Θεσσαλίας–1817 [Athens: Published by the Larissa Municipality, 1989], 192) and Athens (Skoutzes, op. cit., 66ff.).

49. The Peloponnesian example of cooperation and competition among *ayan* and *kocabaşı*s is the best studied case; see M. Sakkelariou, Η Πελοπόννησος

κατά την δεύτερη Τουρκοκρατία (Athens: Verlag der "Byzantinisch-neu-griechischen Jahrbücher", 1939), 96ff., and J.C. Alexander, *Brigandage and Public Order in the Morea* (Athens: Endohora, 1985). For a contemporary Ottoman judgment of the *kocabaşı*s see Süleyman Penah Efendi's *Mecmuası veya Mora ihtilâlı Tarihçesi*, translated by N. Sarris, Προεπαναστατική Ελλάδα και Οσμανικό Κράτος. Από το χειρόγραφο του Σουλευμάν Πενάχ Εφέντη του Μοραΐτη *1785* (Athens: Herodotos, 1993), 293–96. A Peloponnesian himself and a member of the central state elite, Süleyman Pehah Efendi was particularly ill-disposed toward these groups. Multiple other such cases are observed in Greece, especially in the realm of Ali Paşa Tepeleden; see W.W. Leake, *Travels in Northern Greece*, (London: J. Rodwell, 1835), vol. 4, 518.

50. See B. McGowan, *The Economic Life of Ottoman Europe* (Cambridge: Cambridge University Press, 1981), 135–41.

51. G.Veinstein, "Le patrimoine foncier de Panayote Benakis, kocabaşı de Kalamata," *Journal of Turkish Studies* 11 (1987): 211–33.

52. See Petmezas, *Recherches . . .* 601ff., and idem., "Patterns of Proto-industrialization in the Ottoman Empire: The Case of Eastern Thessaly, ca. 1750–1860," *Journal of European Economic History* 19, no. 3 (1990): 575–603.

53. The fourteen communities that formed the Argalast Mukataası 1) paid all their "ordinary" taxes in lump sum (*maktu*), 2) were subjected to the juridical authority of the distant *kadı* of Izdin, 3) were exempted from all extraordinary levies and the *tayin* expenses resulting from visits of Ottoman officials, other than the Argalast Mukataası Voyvodası, and 4) were not to be subjected to any kind of extraordinary levies (like the *avarız, mukabale, nüzül*, and *hane* taxes), with the sole exception of an *avarız*-type impost called *kara astarı*, which was paid in lump sum as an *ocaklık* for the Janissaries in Constantinople. See N. Pantazopoulos, Κοινοτικος βίος εις την Θεσσαλομαγνησίαν επί Τουρκοκρατίας (Salonica: Aristoteleion Panepistimion Thessalonikis, 1967), 66–70.

54. On the distinction between "internal" and "external" fiscal and financial echelons, see above, pages 89 and 91.

55. The *Register of communal finances of Zagora, 1754–1822* (henceforth RCFZ) is kept in the municipal library of Zagora. It was uncatalogued when I copied it back in 1979. The pages for the years 1786–87 had been removed before it was donated to the municipal library.

56. I have estimated the total sum of annual expenses and revenues by adding a "computed" *cizye* (estimated as equal to the 16% to the total sum of expenses, *cizye* excluded, as in 1793/94).

57. In other localities the extra-agricultural sources of revenue were also taken in consideration. In the island of Patmos, for instance, a detailed register of agricultural property was kept and used to distribute the total imposed contribution among individual households. A second list was also kept. It was a roster

of allotment that was used to evaluate total fiscal capacity of each individual household; cf. Asdrachas, "Νησιώτικες Κοινότητες . . ." 26–30. The extra-agricultural sources of revenue were nevertheless rarely registered in detail. I know of no such example of a detailed register.

58. The most prominent of these notable families had business branches in Constantinople, where a guild of woollen stuff fabricants from Pelion was established.

59. Cf. *RCFZ*, f. 1r.

60. Steward of the imperial harem.

61. For an estimation of the aggregate rate of devaluation and depreciation (3% yearly) of the silver *guruş* in 1775–1822, see Petmezas, *Recherches . . .*, 774–79.

62. See notes 67–69 and 72 below.

63. Communal expenditure in 1783/84 was 16,947 constant *guruş*, or a quarter of the communal debt in 1754. See the index of the Ottoman silver *guruş* devaluation relative to the Venetian golden ducat in table 3.

64. It is noteworthy that the same Jewish bankers of Larissa (Yenisehir-i Fener), the Sitoglus and Sarrafoglu, advanced money to the community when necessary. Their bonds (*tahvil*), bearing a relatively high interest (20%), were usually sold to Ottoman women, who were probably looking for a solid investment.

65. See S. Petmezas, "Διαχείριση των κοινοτικών οικονομικών και κοινωνική κυριαρχία. Η στρατηγική των προυχόντων: Ζαγορά 1784–1822," *Mnemon* 13 (1991): 98–99.

66. Cf. *RCFZ*, f. 3.

67. In 1756 at the latest, twenty at least of a total of twenty-eight Pelion communities were subjected to the *kadı* of Izdin, six to that of Platina (Platamon), one to that of Ermiye (Almyros) and another to that of Leivadia; cf. Pantazopoulos, op. cit., 68.

68. The customs tax (*gümrük*) was the only tax which was either farmed separately or of which I did not find any reference in the communal accounts. It was probably paid directly in the customs office of Volos. Earlier in the eighteenth century, when the community was engaged in maritime activities, there had been a customs office in Zagora, but it was in ruins in 1815; see A. Philippidis, Τα περισωθέντα έργα του Αργύρη Φιλιππίδη. Μερική Γεωγραφία—Βιβλίον Ηθικόν (Athens: [s.n.], 1978), 191. The various taxes on livestock husbandry (*resm-i otlak* or *nomistron* and the *celep*) were insignificant in value.

69. The *mal-i maktu* was an aggregated sum that was supposed to include various agricultural taxes; cf. İnalcık, "Fiscal and Military . . .," 333–36.

70. The *kara astar* was an *avarız* type of tax, paid as a substitute for the silk caps that silk-producing villages, like those of Pelion, were supposed to offer to the

Janissaries and the marines (*levendler*) of the Ottoman Fleet; cf. V. Sfyroeras, Τα Ελληνικά πληρώματα του Τουρκικού στόλου (Athens, 1968), 97–99.

71. The *iştira* was an extraordinary tax, paid during the war years as in 1754 (1,770 *guruş*), 1770–73, and 1783/1784–1791/92. After that time it ceased to be paid in Zagora. This is probably due to its suppression in 1793–1807 and its substitution by a new method of grain purchase for the consumption of Istanbul, controlled by the *Zahire Nezareti*; see T. Güran, "The Role of the State in the Grain Supply of Istanbul: The Grain Administration, 1793–1839," *International Journal of Turkish Studies* 3, no. 1 (1984–85): 30–31. In 1810/11, Velyuldin Paşa, governor of Trikkala once again imposed the *iştira* on Zagora as an annual regular contribution.

72. Starting in 1792/93, a new lump sum tax, the *resm-i zacriye* (*krasonomi, krasiatiko*), was imposed. It was an excise tax on the consumption of alcohol, controlled by the newly founded *irade-i cedid* and destined to finance the new model army (*nizam-ı cedid*) of Selim III. This administration showed an extraordinary ability to recover the losses due to *guruş* devaluation.

73. Beginning in 1806 the *resm-i mizan-ı harir* was collected by the administration of the newly founded *tersane-i âmire*, which was also used to finance the military reforms of Selim III; cf. Y. Cezar, *Osmanlı Maliyesinde Bunalım ve Değişim Dönemi (XVIII. yy'dan Tanzimat'a Mali Tarih)* (Istanbul: Alan Yayıncılık, 1986), 216–24. It devolved rapidly under the control of the provincial governors, who had been assigned (*deruhde*) the tax-farming of various taxes which had been (rightly or wrongly) considered unattractive by tax-farmers. It is possible that this *bedel-i harir* of Zagora was assigned to Velyuldin Paşa, who had been already able to acquire the *malikâne mukataası* of Zagora, to raise the fixed lump sum of other taxes he received and to impose new ordinary imposts and extraordinary levies on the community.

74. Cf. İnalcık, "Fiscal and Military . . . .," 335–37. The *harc-ı vilayet* was a provincial tax widely levied in the eighteenth century to meet local expenses; cf. E. Radousev, "Les dépenses locales dans l'empire ottoman au XVIIIe s. (selon les données de registres de cadi de Ruse, Vidin et Sofia)," *Études Balkaniques* 16, no. 3 (1980): 92. It is linked to the rise of the *ayan*: McGowan, op. cit., 158. In the case of Zagora it was destined for the provincial treasury in Larissa. In 1754 the sum paid was very high (4,250 *guruş*). Later, during the war with Russia in 1770–72, it was again relatively important (fluctuating between 1,250 and 1,700 *guruş*). Since 1783 it fell to a lump sum of only 500 *guruş*.

75. The *umur-i şeri* (or *mürasele*) was a light lump-sum tax paid to the *kadı* of Izdin. A small sum of 30–50 *guruş* as a salary for the *naib* was sometimes added. It is probably the equivalent of the *bad-ı hava* and *cürm ve ceremeyn* windfall taxes, collected and kept by the community.

76. After 1789/90 it was a relatively modest annual gift (*pişkeş*), in cash and kind

(2 *okka* of silk), sent to "our efendi Abdeddin Beğ in Larissa." A welcome gift (*ikram*) and extraordinary levies for war preparation (*seferiye*) for the same lord, or for people related to him, like his *Kehya* or an unnamed woman living in Volos, are sometimes added. In 1816/17 this gift was discontinued, probably because Abdeddin Beğ had been exiled from Larissa due to his opposition to Ali Paşa Tepeleden.

77. In 1798/99 the guild of Zagoriot woollen stuff fabricants working at Pera spent 2,445 *guruş* to secure for their community the protection of Hadice Sultan, sister of Selim III. From 1800/01 to 1808/09 an annual gift (*pişkeş*) was sent to the Sultan (750 g.), her *kehya* (350 g.), her *kâtip* (100 g.), and her *kapı çohadarı* (100 g.). It is probable that Hadice Sultan had been the possessor of the tax-farm (*mukataa iltizamı*) sub-farmed by the community. This gift reappeared in 1818/19, when 5,211 g. were given to "*our Sultan thanks to the charity of our lord*" (Velyuddin Paşa).

78. This is an aggregated sum of local expenses for the maintenance of the residence and other necessities of the accommodation of the *malikâne sahibi* or the *amil*.

79. A strong local militia of *martolos*, under the *derbentçi başı* Athanasios Basdekis, protected the Pelion region. There was also a small militia, which protected the coast from pirates.

80. It is known that in the seventeenth and eighteenth centuries in some Greek islands the *cizye* was locally collected by communal officers according to their own criteria, as in Andros in 1721 (D. Dimitropoulos, "Οικογένεια και φορολογικές καταστιχώσεις στα νησιά του Αιγίου κατά την Οθωμανική περίοδο" *Historica* 14 [1997]: 339), in Syros in 1753–86 and in Patmos in 1670–1700 (Asdrachas "Νησιώτικες Κοινότητες . . .," 26 and 31). The vast majority of the population was ranked of the middle group (*evsat*). Poorer members were exempted from paying the *cizye*; see E. Balta, "Le rôle de l'institution communautaire dans la répartition verticale de l'impôt: l'exemple de Santorini au XVIIe siècle," in idem., *Problèmes et approches de l'Histoire ottomane* (Istanbul: Les Editions Isis, 1997), 106–108. In Zagora on average one third of all assessed *cizye* in the years 1783–94 was in arrears.

81. Contributions were proportional to the estimated value of yearly agricultural production. The unpredicted rise of expenses did not lead to the rise of these contributions, which (expressed in constant *guruş*) show a clear cyclical movement; see Petmezas, *Recherches . . .*, 361.

82. Until 1798/99 the treasurer did not differentiate between the "profit and loss" and the uncollected arrears, which were a kind of credit extended to those households that were unable to meet their financial obligations. The eventual profit and the uncollected arrears were transferred to the next year's use revenues. This distinction, introduced in 1799, was an additional evidence of the

sophistication of communal finance management.

83. Cf. Petmezas, *Recherches* . . ., 124–38.

84. Cf. Petmezas, *Recherches* . . ., 393–415, and idem., "Διαχείριση . . .," 93–100.

85. See Petmezas, *Recherches* . . ., 404–406. Some prominent community members lent the community substantial sums of money, whose interest was in perpetuity earmarked for specific charitable purposes (salaries of teachers, scholarships, relief for the poor, etc.).

86. Trikkeri is a quasi-insular community (and was thus one of the possessions of the Kapudan Paşa), which profited from its loyalty to the Ottoman side during the Russian Aegean Expedition in 1770–74 and was granted the privilege of exclusive transport of the *iştira* tax of Thessaly to Istanbul; Petmezas, *Recherches* . . ., 97–99.

87. See Petmezas, *Recherches* . . ., 243–44. The document was graciously provided by Mrs. Ioanna Beopoulou, who is writing on a book on the ethnography of Trikkeri.

88. Cf. Sfyroeras, op. cit., 93–96 and 102. The Ottoman navy was supposed to pay the salaries of the sailors and captains. The community regularly paid an important additional salary and other expenses for its sailors.

89. In 1778, Sultan Abdülhamid I recompensed the loyalty and services of Hydra by assigning to the commune the *iltizam* of the island as a lump sum; see A. Lignos, Αρχείον της κοινότητος Ύδρας (1778–1832), 16 vols. (Athens: Typois Ephem. Sphairas, 1921), 1:1–5. All taxes (except for the *cizye*) were expressed in lump sums. A yearly lump payment to the admiralty of about 2,500 *guruş*, in the beginning of the nineteenth century, comprised a host of taxes and levies: the *resm-i zacriye* (245 *g.*), the *menzil* tax (300 *g.*), the *hediye pahası* (1,250 *g.*), the *zahire pahası* (250 *g.*), an *ikramiye* (100 *g.*) and other small dues to the staff of the Kapudan Paşa; see ibid., 2:162 ; 2:266, 5:124 ; 5:202. A second yearly lump payment comprised the *bedel-i iltizam* (1,000 *g.*), paid in advance (*pesinet*). The aggregate sum fluctuated between 1,500 and 1,900 *guruş*. It was Hydra's part of a larger *mal-i maktu* tax paid by the islands of the Naxa-Para Mukataası to the treasury of the Kapudan Paşa; see ibid., 1:102; 2:346–48; 2:371; 4:10; 5:19; 5:247. See also G.D. Criésis, *Histoire de l'île d'Hydra* (Paris: Imp. H. Chassefiere fils, 1888), 146–47.

90. Mariners and captains of Hydra had the right to buy their *cizye teskeresi* away from home. It is noteworthy that Ottoman officials (*zâbit*), who were responsible for collecting the head tax in the towns of Morea and in Athens, used to withhold the respective *cizye* receipts (*teskere*) from the local peasants (who rarely voyaged) and sell them a second time (for half the price) to the mariners of Hydra and other islands; cf. Skoutzes, op. cit., 103.

91. One levy (*dosimo*) was raised on the owners of large vessels (*karavia*) and another on the owners of smaller ships (*kayık*s and schooners). In 1806 there were 73 large ship owners and 13 schooner owners (Lignos, op. cit., 2:403–407). In 1811 there were 61 large vessels and 47 schooners (ibid., 4:129–30). In 1810–16 this levy was expressly termed as a duty tax (*dazio*) on the products transported (*maksul*) and on the interest of the capital (*diaforo sermayias*) invested in these ships.

92. A levy was raised on the shopkeepers and on the owners of bakeries, windmills, and horse-powered mills.

93. *Tansa* derives from the Italian word *tassa*, meaning tax; see Balta, op. cit., 99. The word was used in most islands of the Archipelago and in some parts of the Greek mainland. Cf. S. Asdrachas, "Πραγματικότητες από τον ιη," Σταθμοί προς την νέα Ελληνική Κοινωνία (Athens: Epoches, 1965), 12. In Patmos (Asdrachas, "Νησιώτικες Κοινότητες . . ." 28–30) and Serifos (Liata, op. cit., 111–17) registers of *tansa* assessment were prepared according to locally specific criteria, usually founded on agricultural property and sometimes on other non-agricultural sources of income.

94. See table 7. The source is Lignos, op. cit., 1:99; 2:92–96, 202–206, 324–30, 469–75; 3:200–201, 389–94, 566–72; 4:120–28, 218–28; 5:16–18, 91–93, 186–88, 244–46; 6:608–635.

95. The Zagorya *nahiyesi* was a group of 46 mountainous communities, 30 kilometers from Ioannina, the main income of which was provided by animal husbandry, wool industry, and temporary emigration of its inhabitants as artisans and merchants to urban centers like Ioannina and Istanbul. All but three were *timar* holdings, but the *sipahi*s were contented with an annual lump sum payment (*kesim*), to which some symbolically important dues in kind were added. They also received the *tapu kesimi* for every land transaction; see Papageorgiou, op. cit., 74–75.

96. Faltaits, op. cit.

97. See Sakellariou, op. cit., 90–92.

98. See Süleyman Penah, op. cit., 261–63.

99. See T. Kandiloros, "Απολογισμός των εσόδων και εξόδων της Γορτυνίας επι Τουρκοκρατίας," *Arkadike Epeteris* (1906): 312–22. This document is a part of the Deliyiannis family archive; See K. Gardika, "Δανεισμος και φορολογια στα χωρια της Καρυταινας, 1817–1821," Δελτίο του Κέντρου Ερεύνης της Ιστορίας του Νεώτερου Ελληνισμού 1 (1998): 67–80.

100. Among them the *mal-i miri*, the *cizye*, the *resm-i zacriye*, the *celep*, the *menzil*, and various *tekâlif-i örfiye* and *tekâlif-i sakka*. According to Gardika (op.cit., 71–73) some of the regular taxes and levies—e.g. those related to the *malikâne* revenues of the *kaza* held by Beyhan Sultan, sister of Selim III—were not in-

cluded in this document. If this is true we must assume that the real per capita tax burden was higher.

101. See Papageorgiou, op. cit., 189.

102. See Papageorgiou, op. cit., 44–50 and 155–58.

103. There are only three cases of villages transformed to *çiftlik*s and two of them ended up as monastic properties; see Papageorgiou, op. cit., 25–32.

104. See Papageorgiou, op. cit., 152–53 and 231–33.

105. See Salzman, "An Ancien Régime . . .," 407–408.

106. See in the Communal Library of Miliais, Λυτά έγγραφα, folder no. 7, document no. 8 (catalogued by V. Skouvaras).

107. Traian Stoianovich ("Αγρότες και γαιοκτήμονες στο Οθωμανικό Κράτος: οικογενειακή οικονομία,οικονομία της αγοράς και εκσυγχρονισμός," in Εκσυγχρονισμός και Βιομηχανική Επανάσταση στα Βαλκάνια [Athens: Themelio, 1980], 172–73) has made comparable estimations on the per capita imposition in the Ottoman Empire. According to his estimates a *reaya* household head would have to pay 44 *guruş* annually in 1794 (24.1 constant *g*.). He also calculated that a quarter of the economic output of the Peloponnese was captured in the form of taxes and levies and considered that the population of the Ottoman Empire, less developed economically than that of Europe, bore a relatively higher tax burden.

108. See Petmezas, *Recherches* . . ., 254. It covers the aggregate taxation of Pelion, and possibly excludes expenses for the local administration. In that case the figure is not comparable to the others and should be corrected by a 20% increase (31 guruş per household).

109. The number of households and the correction coefficients for the Pelion communities are taken from Petmezas, *Recherches* . . ., 132–35. Data for Trikkeri were corrected for an estimated 12-month budget. Those for Karytaina *kazası* are taken from V. Panayiotopoulos Πληθυσμός της Πελοποννήσου στην Τουρκοκρατία (Athens, 1985), 324–26, for Morea from Stoianovich (loc. cit.) and for Hydra from August de Jassaud, *Mémoire sur l'état physique et politique des isles d'Hydra, Spécie, Poro et Ipséra en l'année 1808* (Athens: Librairie N. Karavias, 1978), 11 and 33. The correction coefficients for the *vakıflı* villages, Karytaina, or the Morea are just indicative and should be used with great caution. I have chosen not to include the available detailed data on the island of Samos for the years 1808–12 (A. Sevastakis, Το κίνημα των καρμανιόληδων στη Σάμο, 1805–1812. Με ανέκδοτα έγγραφα [Athens: Pneumatiko Hidryma Samou "Nikolaos Demetriou", 1996]) because a large part of taxes and levies were directly collected by tax collectors and were not included in the published registers of communal expenses. The registered average annual tax burden was 30,450 constant *g*. and the unknown real tax burden

may be twice this sum. European travellers of the beginning of the nineteenth century gave contradictory information on the total population of the island that ranged between 12,000 and 60,000 inhabitants.

Jewish Enlightenment and Nationalism in the Ottoman Balkans: Barukh Mitrani in Edirne in the Second Half of the Nineteenth Century

ARON RODRIGUE

Westernization, the Haskalah (Jewish Enlightenment) movement, and Jewish nationalism all emerged as significant trends among the Jewish communities of the Ottoman Balkans in the modern period. The career and publications of the educator and writer, Barukh ben Isaac Mitrani, an important figure in the Ottoman city of Edirne, throw much light on these new cultural and intellectual developments. Religious messianic ideas as well as modern Haskalah ones combined in the case of Mitrani to put him squarely in the camp of the fledgling movement of religious Zionism.

The contributions of Mitrani to the Hebrew press of his time have been noted and analyzed, most notably by Shelomoh Haramati.[1] This article will focus on his Judeo-Spanish publications, as well as on his letters in Hebrew to the Alliance Israélite Universelle, to complement this study and to place him and his work within the larger context of the Judeo-Spanish world in full transition and mutation in the second half of the nineteenth century.

Judeo-Spanish-speaking communities constituted a distinctive culture area in the Ottoman Empire, covering most of the Turkish Balkans and the littoral of the Aegean sea.[2] Edirne Jewry, with a population of 8–10,000 in the middle of the nineteenth century, was an important community in this region, and had played an important role in the history of Ottoman Jewry dating back to the period when the city was the capital of the early Empire. The city was at the heart of Turkish Rumeli, and was situated at the crossroads of trade routes from the West and the North to Istanbul and to Salonica. It was an important center of regional trade. While most Jews were shopkeepers and artisans, the richest families were involved with commerce in textiles, animal skins, and colonial produce.[3]

The Edirne Jewish community was a traditional one, with two rabbinical dynasties, the Geron and the Behmoiras, ruling over thirteen synagogues named after the various areas of the Iberian peninsula, Italy, and Central Europe from which the Jews had come in waves beginning in the fourteenth century. The overwhelming majority of the population was made up of Sephardim who had arrived following the expulsions from the Iberian peninsula.[4]

An important opening of the community to the wider movements of change affecting European Jewry can be dated with the arrival in the city of the noted *maskil* (participant in the Haskalah movement) and Hebraist, Joseph Halevi. It was the movement that he engendered locally that provides the backdrop for Mitrani's writings and activities.

There has been controversy about the personal and intellectual background of Halevi, who was to make a name for himself later as an Orientalist scholar in Paris. He became famous in the Jewish world after the Alliance sent him to Ethiopia in 1867 to investigate the Falashas. While there is considerable evidence that he was an Ashkenazi Jew from Hungary, his origins remain shrouded in mystery.[5]

While Narcisse Leven claimed that Halevi founded a new school in Edirne in 1850,[6] an account by Halevi states that he started to be active in public life there in 1856.[7] The later date seems likely, as it is also confirmed by another account of his arrival.[8] His considerable learning in Hebrew and the Talmud led to his initial acceptance by the rabbinical corps of the town, and he was taken under the wing of Rabbi Bekhor Danon, the secretary to the Chief Rabbi and the father of Abraham Danon, a noted *maskil* in his own right a generation later, and the director of the first modern rabbinical seminary in the Ottoman Empire.[9] Halevi became the director of the Talmud Torah (the major Jewish school) of the Portuguese congregation of the town, one of the thirteen congregations that made up the Jewish community. He put great stress upon the learning of Hebrew according to the rules of grammar, a move dear to the heart of European *maskilim*, and created reading societies which subscribed to the European Hebrew press. This was to be a step pregnant with consequences, as this press was to emerge as a very important conduit for new ideas flowing between the Ashkenazi and Sephardi worlds.

Halevi slowly began to introduce reforms at his school, starting to teach Hebrew grammar systematically and introducing the teaching of French. A group of reformers coalesced around him and managed to bring about the fusion of the many small schools into one big Talmud Torah with Halevi as its director. However, opposition soon made itself manifest, especially around the issue of the teaching of French and his ideas about the need to radically reform Jewish society and education by stressing European learning. The opposition proved to be too strong to overcome, and Halevi had to abandon Edirne. His experiment had lasted five years and had sown the seeds of the Haskalah and the revival of Hebrew in the city.[10]

Halevi was also to play a crucial role in the foundation of the Alliance Israélite Universelle school there, the first long-lasting and the most successful of the institutions of the Alliance network in the Judeo-Spanish culture area.[11] His activities illustrate the significance of the preparation by *maskilim* of the way for the successful implantation of Alliance schools in the Judeo-Spanish communities in the major centers.

By the middle of the 1860s, Halevi had returned to Edirne and managed to re-open a small school run according to his ideas. Aware of the foundation of the Alliance through the European Hebrew press, he began to recruit members for the organization, and informed the Central Committee, in a letter written in Hebrew, of the creation of a provincial Alliance committee for Rumeli.[12]

Halevi's work in the 1850s hence had borne some fruit. There was a small group in town which had come under his influence and was in touch with Haskalah ideas through the reading of Hebrew newspapers such as *Ha-Magid*.[13] This group came to be associated with the local Alliance committee created by Halevi. It was this group that invited the Alliance in 1867 to take over Halevi's school. This invitation is almost a prototype of the letters the Alliance would receive in the next decades from local communities, inviting it either to send directors to already existing schools or to open new ones:

> We, the undersigned, directors of the Jewish school of Edirne called the *Talmud Torah `im derekh erez* (the study of Torah combined with secular knowledge), convinced of the necessity of giving a good French education to our students in order to introduce them to European civilization, beg the very honorable Central Committee of the Alliance Israélite Universelle to give its valued assistance by providing us with a suitable teacher for the teaching of the French language and of the elements of modern sciences . . . [We hope that] the Alliance will not delay in coming to the help of numerous coreligionists who, awakened from an age-old and enervating lethargy, begin at last to open their eyes to the light of civilization with the aim of becoming useful citizens and enlightened defenders of the ideas of liberty and humanity which have been proclaimed so solemnly by our holy religion.[14]

The letter guaranteed a local subsidy of 2,000 French francs a year for three years, and agreed to all the stipulations that the Alliance might wish to make. Among the signatories were two traders in colonial produce (Salomon Bekhor Eliakim, Samuel Pisa), one broker in cereals and wool (Yohai Nardea), one rabbi (Elia Navon), and one accountant in the banking house of Moïse de Toledo (Joseph Suhami). Only the latter knew French, having been educated in Marseilles, and had in fact been the French teacher of Joseph Halevi.[15]

In the meantime, Halevi had become well-known to the Alliance leadership, having traveled to Paris and having convinced it of his qualifications to pursue a mission to the Falashas to inquire into their situation. On his way to Africa, stopping in Edirne in 1867, he was quick to second the request of his followers. He waxed ecstatic over the changes that he saw in the Edirne Jewish community:

> The dissensions that reigned since the awakening of the people, between the secularist partisans of progress and the con-

servative casuists (the hakhamim), have ended with the total defeat of the latter and everybody wishes an enlightened education for their children. The fanaticism . . . which causes such devastation within the communities of northeastern Europe is thankfully unknown among the exiled from the Iberian peninsula. Once one manages to shake the laziness . . . which the climate of this country seems to engender, our co-religionists embrace progress from which no refined casuistry can separate them . . .[16]

The Alliance accepted the invitation and sent Félix Bloch, a recent Alsatian graduate of the Paris Rabbinical Seminary, to head the school.

In one of his letters to the Alliance, Halevi mentioned an old student of his who was now "an excellent teacher of religion . . . teaching the Bible and Hebrew grammar following the rules of a manuscript I left him."[17] This was Barukh Mitrani.

Mitrani was born in Edirne in 1847. His father Isaac Mitrani was a Hebrew teacher who passed a deep love of the language to his son. Father and son were both deeply influenced by Halevi, and it was Isaac Mitrani who was selected to direct Halevi's school upon his departure from Edirne, Barukh becoming the Hebrew teacher in the same school.[18]

Barukh Mitrani soon emerged as a polemicist. He published violent critiques of traditional Jewish education in Judeo-Spanish newspapers such as the *Jurnal Israelit*[19] of Istanbul criticizing its lack of method and grammar. He himself published a textbook of Hebrew with Judeo-Spanish explanations which he hoped would be adopted as a textbook by the Jewish schools of the Levant.[20]

He was well acquainted with Haskalah ideas and published extensively in the Hebrew press. However, his *maskilic* outlook notwithstanding, and in spite of his support for modern education, he soon came into conflict with the Alliance. His father had been retained as a teacher of Hebrew in the Alliance school in Edirne. He himself had to move to Shumla (present day Shumen in Bulgaria), where he taught Hebrew in the newly opened Alliance school during 1869–1870.[21] He came back to Edirne at the end of this period, and wanted to become the director of the new girls' school opened by Bloch, the director of the Alliance institution in the town. Not receiving much encouragement, he proceeded to open a rival school for girls. Bloch, of course, did not receive this very well.[22]

Throughout the early 1870s, Mitrani remained in communication with the Alliance. He and Bloch quarreled and made up many times. The tug-of-war between them over the control of the girls' school continued until after Bloch's departure in 1873. In the end, Mitrani published several vitriolic diatribes against Alliance teachers in the Hebrew press of the time, in newspapers such as *Havazelet* and *Ha-Magid*, accusing the teachers of diverging from the original path of the organization, desecrating the Sabbath, giving more importance to French than to Hebrew, and looking down on the people.[23] He reiterated these accusations in long letters in flowing Hebrew to the Central Committee. For him, the origins of all the evil sprang from the faulty education received in the Alliance teacher training institution in Paris, the École Normale Israélite Orientale.[24]

Mitrani founded a society with over two hundred members, the Mikveh Yisrael, which supported the new school directed by him and his father, and bombarded the Alliance from 1874 on with letters requesting a teacher of French, and financial help. It is interesting to note that his ideal heroes were Eastern European *maskilim* with whose writings he had become acquainted through his reading of the Hebrew press. He wanted Jewishly observant teachers, enlightened *maskilim* such as Haim Selig Slonimsky and Abraham Beer Gottlober, who would teach foreign languages but would not transform the school into a French institution.[25]

The Alliance at first tried to conciliate Mitrani, and then ignored him. Mitrani was too demanding for the Alliance to enter into any kind of long-lasting relationship with him. Furthermore, it did not like being attacked publicly, and responded in the way that it would always respond to such attacks, with silence. It stood by its teachers.

Mitrani did not have a real power base in the Edirne community, was hated by the Alliance local committee as well as the traditionalist rabbinate,[26] and soon had to close his school for financial reasons. He left the town sometime in the late 1870s.[27] He was active in journalism in the Balkans, Vienna, and Palestine in the following decade.

This was the golden age of the Judeo-Spanish press in the Empire, which had emerged in tandem with the birth of modern journalism among all the major peoples under Ottoman rule. The opening of the horizons of Sephardi

Jewry in the second half of the nineteenth century led to an explosion of journalistic and literary activity. Given the fact that the mass constituency was still largely Judeo-Spanish speaking, this activity emerged primarily in this language. Istanbul, Izmir, and Salonika became centers of Judeo-Spanish publishing. David Fresko's *El Tiempo* and Izak Gabay's *El Telegrafo*, newspapers founded in the 1870s in Istanbul propagandized aggressively for modernization. These two Istanbul newspapers became dailies in the 1880s and continued to publish until the 1930s. Aron Hazan's *La Buena Esperansa* and Alexander Ben Giat's *El Meseret* in Izmir, and Saadi Halevi's *La Epoca* in Salonica also became important periodicals.[28] Reporting on news in the Jewish and non-Jewish worlds, translating, adapting European works of fiction and non-fiction, the Judeo-Spanish press was, in many ways, the progenitor of modern Sephardi politics and culture.

Mitrani was a prolific letter writer to all these newspapers and tried his hand at newspaper publishing himself. He had returned to Edirne in the 1880s, left again for Palestine, and then wandered around from city to city in Bulgaria. In 1881 he published a Hebrew and Judeo-Spanish newspaper called *Karmi* where he expounded his ideas on the re-awakening of the Jewish people. This venture collapsed soon thereafter. He made another attempt to live off his writings with the publication of a Judeo-Spanish newspaper, the *Karmi Sheli*, in 1890–1891. But this also failed, and Mitrani retired from public life, dying at the age of 72 in Edirne in 1919.

The conflict between Mitrani and Bloch and other Alliance teachers was unique in that the opposition to the organization came from the quarter in which it was used to having friends, that of the *maskilim*. The feud was sparked by the personal grievances of Mitrani, who was excluded by Bloch from a position in the schools in Edirne. But one should also note the great ideological differences between the position of Mitrani and that espoused by the organization. The latter wanted to "regenerate" Eastern Jewry in order to remake it in the image of the "enlightened" sections of French Jewry, into honorable citizens, proud of their religion but also fully conversant with "civilization"—that is, Western, especially French, civilization. Barukh Mitrani, though sharing the critique of traditional Jewish education, had a very different goal in mind.

For Mitrani, the aim of the education in the schools was to strengthen Judaism through correct education, not to weaken it, as he accused the Alliance of doing. This would be achieved through emphasizing Hebrew education, by the usage of Hebrew as a living language in the schools, as the primary language of instruction. French and Turkish would follow as secondary languages.[29] Hence it was important to have teachers who would obey all the religious commandments, would be fluent in Hebrew and would not dethrone its primary place in education.[30] Furthermore, it was important for the Alliance and its teachers to observe local traditions and customs and not to weaken them through excessive Europeanization, as the result would ultimately be the perdition of Judaism.[31]

This primacy given to Hebrew by Mitrani has to be understood within the context of the primarily ideological divergence of his views from those espoused by the Alliance. Whereas the organization worked for the "regeneration" of the individual Jew through the process of European education that would prepare him for the benefits of emancipation, Mitrani's ideal was the national regeneration and emancipation of the Jewish people as a collectivity through their ultimate restoration in the Holy Land. The two ideologies, though both critical of traditional Jewish society, were in fact diametrically opposed as to the final outcome.

Mitrani first outlined his worldview in his Judeo-Spanish book, *Diskorso de Perashat Shemot*, published in Salonica in 1869. The starting point of this work is the great revolution brought about by the process of emancipation of the Jews in the West, the changing attitude of the nations towards the "chosen people." This was brought about by the spread of "civilization," which was of great benefit for the Jews. However, the Jews were not taking advantage of this new set of circumstances and remained mired in obscurantism and fanaticism. The lack of education was the principal cause of the backwardness of the Jews compared to the advances made by other nations.[32] Listing all the traditional reasons to account for their dispersion, Mitrani added that salvation was impossible if the Jews did not gather their forces. "The sacred language is not well known . . . [and we] lack science and the arts of government [*artifisios de reinado*] . . . . As long as we are lazy, Judaism is weak, the sacred language is unknown and there is no education, God is right to castigate us and to leave us in *Galut* [exile]."[33] His book was intended as an appeal to the Jewish nation, to "awaken it from the sleep of fanaticism and to make it understand what the Law, science and the civilized times of today requires from us."[34] If the nations of the world who did not even have the benefit of the holy law could advance so, how could the "chosen People" remain behind? Schools and more schools were needed where science and the "rules of civilization" would be taught, and the sacred language learnt well. Only with this learning would "the arts of government [*artifisios de reinado*]" be acquired again and then "we will be redeemed and saved, and settled in the Holy Land, prosperous with the *melekh ha-mashiyah*."[35]

Strongly reminiscent of Yehudah Alkalai, another Sephardi Jew who was one of the earliest figures of religious Zionism, who was based in neighboring Serbia, and whom he cited many times in his publications,[36] Mitrani stressed the importance of human activism in the here and now to bring about the messianic age and the restoration of the Jews. He is unique, however, in the Judeo-Spanish world, in emphasizing the primordial importance of the acquisition of modern skills for this process to take place. Modern education and traditional Judaism coexist in complete harmony in his worldview. The admixture of traditional messianic ideas, orthodox religious practice, and modern *maskilic* notions about the importance of worldly education in Mitrani's thought foreshadow many of the strands that would go into the making of modern religious Zionism at the end of the century.

One of the running themes in Mitrani's thought, developed first in his *Diskorso* and then in his other writings, is the awakening of the nations of Europe, which he attributed to advances in science and civilization. According to Mitrani, writing in the *Karmi* in 1881, humankind had been created by God in the form of nations.[37] The individual, the family, and the nation constituted a common organic whole.[38] Six attributes made for the constitution of a nationality: 1. the family, common descent; 2. a common past; 3. a country; 4. the law; 5. the language; 6. customs.[39] Peoples who had even two or three of these attributes were claiming to be nations. All the more reason for the Jews to come forth with their claims, as they were the first nation, and had all six of these attributes.[40]

But the Jews had fallen behind, as they were asleep in fanaticism. Mitrani was fierce in his attacks on the traditionalists who rejected science and civilization. The latter two, according to him, were "clean" and "honest" and were not responsible for those Jews who abandoned Judaism. This was due to faulty education in the family.[41] There was no contradiction between the law (which he called *la santa ley liberala*) and modern civilization. In 1891, in the *Karmi Sheli*, he cited approvingly the founder of modern neo-Orthodox Judaism, the German leader Samson Raphael Hirsch, for his arguments proving this point.[42]

However, the harmony between the law and civilization did not mean that one could abandon the commandments. Only a new Sanhedrin in the Holy Land could change the law.[43] He had now grown wary of the so-called "civilized" among the Jews after his quarrel with the Alliance teachers. According to Mitrani, the holy law was one of the foundation stones of Jewish nationality, and should be obeyed in full. Disregarding the *mitsvot* (commandments) was, therefore, an attack on Jewish nationalism as well as on the Jewish religion.

Mitrani often bemoaned the fact that he was caught between two sides, the fanatical obscurantists on the one hand and the irreligious radicals on the other. He preferred the middle way, but he also pointed out that in the growing polarization between the two sides, his situation between the rabbis and the "philosophers" was an essentially lonely one.[44]

Mitrani's messianism is indisputable. The awakening of nationalities in Europe and the better treatment of the Jews in Europe with their emancipation were both signs that the messianic era was at hand. The Jews had to "raise" their nation through education, and then God would show them signs of deliverance.[45] Important times were at hand, God was calling the Jews to settle in the Holy Land, and they had to think of the Messiah all the time.[46]

The optimism about the relationship between the nations and the Jews so much in evidence in his *Diskorso* in 1869 had turned darker with the full emergence of antisemitism after the pogroms of the 1880s. Writing in 1891 in the *Karmi Sheli*, Mitrani dwelt at great length on the activities of antisemitic parties and movements in Germany, Austria, and Hungary and took note of Drumont's antisemitic writings.[47] But he saw the finger of God and of the messianic era in this development.[48] Antisemitism was there as a way of turning Jews who had been drifting away from Judaism back into the fold of religion and of heightening their national consciousness.

His messianism, like Alkalai's, had an activist component. The land was of paramount importance to the Jews as a nation and the settlement in the Holy Land could not wait the arrival of the Messiah. The Jews had to learn productive skills and create colonies in the Holy Land; only then would the Messiah arrive. This theme, already apparent in the *Diskorso*, where he highlights the importance for the Jews of acquiring "the art of government," becomes even more important in his writing later. By 1891, he was reporting regularly on settlement societies in the Holy Land throughout the world, but especially in Bulgaria.[49] He urged the Judeo-Spanish communities to take part in this endeavor by creating a colony in honor of their great nationalist thinker, Yehudah Alkalai.[50] The Jews had to reconstitute themselves into a kingdom in the Holy Land under the Ottoman Sultan, and he expected European nations to help them in this task.[51]

Mitrani's writings not only show a great familiarity with the Hebrew press, to which he himself was a frequent contributor, but also demonstrate his exposure to the works of important non-Jewish and Jewish thinkers. In *Karmi*, he cited both Mirabeau and John Stuart Mill in his arguments to prove the overriding importance of national sentiment in human history.[52] There is no evidence to suggest that he read these authors in the original or that his knowledge of their work went beyond expositions of their thought that he might have found in the Hebrew press. Nevertheless, his use of these authors and his reporting of developments in politics and culture outside the Jewish world illustrate the degree to which ideas and news flowed between Europe and the Balkans to affect Sephardi life and thought in the second half of the nineteenth century. The opening to the West brought about the work of *maskilim* such as Halevi, and eventually the Alliance schools, and engendered many new currents among the Sephardim that began to parallel developments in the Ashkenazi communities.

It is clear that Jewish writers and thinkers had the most important impact on Mitrani. Alkalai emerges as an omnipresent figure in his thought and is cited extensively. He is Mitrani's great hero, who was not understood in his time but whose views had now been vindicated.[53] Other Jewish thinkers such as Kalischer and David Gordon are also cited as having influenced his thought.[54] But many others, from Nachman Krochmal to Heinrich Graetz to Samson Raphael Hirsch, figure prominently in his polemics and are quoted at great length.[55] Though operating in a region which on the surface appears as peripheral to the great centers of Jewish life and thought in the nineteenth century, Mitrani emerges as a figure very much at home in the great currents of ideas sweeping European Jewry of the time.

The work of the Alliance appears never to have lost its importance for Mitrani who, in spite of his conflicts with the organization, was still calling it "the merciful mother of Israel" (*la piadoza madre de Israel*) in 1891.[56] As with Alkalai and Kalischer, the foundation of the Alliance had represented the beginning of the new messianic age for Mitrani. It epitomized the galvanization of somnolent Jewish forces. Its work was crucial for the restoration of the Jews through education, and through the acquisition of all the skills of modern civilization. However, the directors of the schools of the organization had perverted the original message and were abandoning religion. The Alliance appeared to have lost control over its personnel. This was why he and his father had to leave the organization.[57] This critique, which prefigured many of the charges levelled against the Alliance by the Zionists two decades later, was a strongly-felt one, which however did not preclude Mitrani from ascribing to the organization an all-important role in the national saga of the restoration of the Jews.

An analysis of Mitrani's work reveals all the various trends that were influential in Edirne and elsewhere in the Balkans in the second half of the nineteenth century. The precedent of the *maskilic* activities of Halevi and the beginning of a Haskalah movement in Edirne, with its strong stress upon the importance and revival of the Hebrew language, had laid the groundwork. Once the movement had emerged in the city, continuous exposure to the Hebrew press of the time had nurtured its development through the propagation of the ideas of the European Haskalah and indeed of the news of broader political and cultural developments elsewhere. The Judeo-Spanish press added to this trend by rendering it more accessible to the masses who could not read Hebrew. The shock of the secularizing work of the Alliance Israélite Universelle, and its ideas of western-style acculturation, emancipation, and assimilation, as well as the reforms that had been undertaken by the Ottoman government beginning with the Tanzimat, all had begun to alter irretrievably the world that the Sephardim had known for centuries. To this was added the fragmentation of the Ottoman Balkans with the rise of nationalism among the various Balkan peoples and the emergence of an independent Bulgaria in 1878, which, unlike the cases of newly independent Serbia and Greece before, now affected a substantial number of Sephardim. The example of nationalism espoused by the neighboring peoples could not but have important consequences for the Jews of the Balkans.

The case of Mitrani is interesting not so much in the influence he had on others in the area—for we know very little about the direct resonance of his particular ideas, except to note the efflorescence of a secularized version of them in Bulgaria where he was active for decades and where modern Zionism would sweep all before it by World War I. But Mitrani is fascinating as a symptom of the Ottoman Sephardi universe in transition, of the mutations that could be engendered by modern developments in the Jewish and non-Jewish worlds in this particular area and of the conjuncture that could give rise to full-blown Zionism in the writings and actions of a highly distinctive individual long before the emergence of the modern Zionist political movement. It also provides a case study of the emergence of Jewish nationalism among the Sephardim that was not just the natural outgrowth of traditional religious yearnings for Zion, as has been claimed many times, but was deeply embedded in all the modern crosscurrents that were to transform the life of all the inhabitants of the Ottoman Empire in the modern period.

Notes

1. Shelomoh Haramati, *Sheloshah she-kadmu le-Ben Yehudah* (Jerusalem: Yad Yitshak Ben-Tsevi, 1978), 48–81.
2. For a general history of this community, see Esther Benbassa and Aron Rodrigue, *Sephardi Jewry: A History of the Judeo-Spanish Community, 14th–20th Centuries* (Berkeley: University of California Press, 2000).
3. A. H. Navon, "Contribution à l'histoire de la fondation des écoles de l'Alliance Israélite Universelle," *Le Judaïsme Sephardi* 1 (July 1932): 8–9.
4. Archives of the Alliance Israélite Universelle, Turquie VII.E., Franco, received in Paris on 10 January 1897.
5. See his obituary in *El Tiempo*, 29 April 1925, where it is stated that he was born in Hungary. There is also other evidence pointing in the direction of his Ashkenazi origins. A. H. Navon mentions that when he arrived in Edirne, he was able to communicate only in Hebrew, implying that he did not know any Judeo-Spanish. See A. H. Navon, "La fondation de l'école de l'Alliance à Andrinople," *Paix et Droit* 3 (April 1923): 13–15. It is inconceivable that a Sephardi Jew in the Balkan peninsula in the middle of the nineteenth century would not know Judeo-Spanish. Halevi's letters in Hebrew to the Alliance are in the Ashkenazi cursive, and not in the Sephardi one common to all the letters in Hebrew sent from the Sephardi communities of the Balkans and Asia Minor. See his file in the Archives of the Alliance Israélite Universelle, Turquie I. J. 1. The question of his origins is discussed also in Haramati, *Sheloshah*, 13, notes 2 and 3.
6. Narcisse Leven, *Cinquante ans d'histoire. L'Alliance Israélite Universelle*

(1860–1910), 2 vols. (Paris: F. Alcan, 1911–1920), 2:67.

7. Joseph Halevi, *Mahberet Melizah ve-Shir* (Jerusalem: Bi-defus A. M. Lunts, 1894), 201.

8. Navon, "La fondation," 13–15.

9. On Danon, see Aron Rodrigue, "The Alliance Israélite Universelle and the Attempt to Reform Rabbinical and Religious Instruction in Turkey," in Simon Schwarzfuchs, ed., *L'"Alliance" dans les communautés du bassin méditerranéen à la fin du 19e siècle et son influence sur la situation sociale et culturelle* (Jerusalem: Misgav Yerushalayim, 1987), LIII–LXX.

10. See Navon, "La fondation," 13–15. See also Haramati, *Sheloshah*, 13–22.

11. For a study of these schools, see Aron Rodrigue, *French Jews, Turkish Jews: The Alliance Israélite Universelle and the Politics of Jewish Schooling in Turkey, 1860–1925* (Bloomington: Indiana University Press, 1990).

12. Archives of the Alliance Israélite Universelle, Turquie I. J. 1, 14 Nisan 5625/1865.

13. A. H. Navon, "Contribution," *Judaïsme Sephardi* 4 (November 1932): 64–66.

14. Archives of the Alliance Israëlite Universelle, Turquie IV. E., letter dated 18 June 1867.

15. A. H. Navon, "Contribution," *Judaïsme Sephardi* 4 (November 1932): 64–66.

16. This quotation is from two letters by Halevi to Paris, both dated 27 June 1867. They are to be found in Archives of the Alliance Israélite Universelle.

17. Archives of the Alliance Israélite Universelle, Turquie I. J. 1, Halevi, 27 June 1867.

18. Haramati, *Sheloshah*, 48.

19. *Jurnal Israelit*, 12 January 1867.

20. Barukh Mitrani, *Sefer Hinukh Banim* (Jerusalem, 1875).

21. Haramati, *Sheloshah*, p. 55.

22. Archives of the Alliance Israélite Universelle, Turquie VI. E., Bloch, 21 September 1871.

23. See for example *Havazelet*, 22 Av 5633/1873.

24. Archives of the Alliance Israélite Universelle, Turquie IV. E., Mitrani, received 16 August 1875.

25. Ibid., received 24 February 1874.

26. Archives of the Alliance Israélite Universelle, Turquie V. E., Bendelac, 26 May 1874.

27. Haramati, *Sheloshah*, p. 48.

28. The Judeo-Spanish press is catalogued in Moshe D. Gaon, *Ha-`Itonut be-Ladino: bibliyografyah: shelosh me'ot `itonim* (A Bibliography of the Judeo-Span-

ish [Ladino] Press) (Jerusalem: Mekhon Ben-Tsevi ba-Universitah ha-`Ivrit, 1965).

29. Archives of the Alliance Israélite Universelle, Turquie IV. E., Mitrani, 24 February 1874.

30. Archives of the Alliance Israélite Universelle, Turquie IV. E., Mitrani, 17 June 1875.

31. Archives of the Alliance Israélite Universelle, Turquie IV. E., Mitrani, 16 August 1875.

32. Barukh Mitrani, *Diskorso de Perashat Shemot* (Salonica, 1868), 42–43.

33. Ibid., 26–27.

34. Ibid., 1.

35. Ibid., 47.

36. *Karmi Sheli* (1891): 4–5.

37. *Karmi* (1881): 6.

38. Ibid., 27.

39. *Karmi* (1881): 49.

40. Ibid.

41. *Karmi Sheli* (1891): 46.

42. Ibid., 71.

43. *Karmi* (1881): 59.

44. Ibid., 62.

45. Ibid., 31.

46. Ibid., 68–69.

47. *Karmi Sheli* (1891): 2–3, 12.

48. Ibid., 5.

49. Ibid., 5, 18.

50. Ibid., 5.

51. *Karmi* (1881): 70, and *Karmi Sheli* (1891): 74.

52. *Karmi* (1881): 29–31.

53. *Karmi Sheli* (1891): 5.

54. Ibid., 60.

55. *Karmi* (1881): 34–34, 38–45; *Karmi Sheli* (1891): 71.

56. *Karmi Sheli* (1891): 12.

57. Ibid., 47.

About the Editor and Contributors

MOLLY GREENE is Director of Graduate Studies and Associate Professor in the History Department, Princeton University. She is the author of *A Shared World: Christians and Muslims in the Early Modern Mediterranean.*

NAJWA AL-QATTAN is Associate Professor of History at Loyola Marymount University in Los Angeles. Her work has focused on the Ottoman Muslim court, dhimmis, and Ottoman memory of the Great War.

FATMA MÜGE GÖÇEK, Associate Professor of Sociology, University of Michigan, has authored and edited several books, including *Rise of the Bourgeoisie, Demise of Empire: Ottoman Westernization and Social Change.*

SOCRATES D. PETMEZAS is Assistant Professor in Modern and Contemporary History at the University of Crete, Gallou campus. His publications include a book in Greek on the history of Greek agriculture in the nineteenth century and a Greek translation of Erik J. Zürcher's *Turkey: A Modern History.*

ARON RODRIGUE is Professor of History and Eva Chernov Lokey Professor in Jewish Studies at Stanford University. He is the author or editor of several books, including *Sephardi Jewry: A History of the Judeo-Spanish Community, 14th–20th Centuries* (with Esther Benbassa).

www.ingramcontent.com/pod-product-compliance
Lightning Source LLC
Chambersburg PA
CBHW020614270326
41927CB00005B/333